Language and Literacy in Uganda

Towards a sustainable reading culture

Editor
Kate Parry

Fountain Publishers

Fountain Publishers Ltd.
P.O. Box 488
Kampala, Uganda

© Department of Language Education, Makerere University 2000
First published 2000

ISBN 9970 02 202 4

Contents

Contributors   iii
Abbreviations   v
Note on publication style   vi
Preface   vii

PART ONE: OVERVIEW
Introduction   1
1. Language and literacy in Uganda: A view from the Ministry
    of Education and Sports   2
    Apolo Nsibambi
2. National policy and practice in language and literature
    education: Some reflections from afar   6
    Gordon P. McGregor

PART TWO: A LANGUAGE FOR NATIONAL COMMUNICATION
Introduction   14
3. A language policy for national integration: Facilitators and
    inhibitors   16
    Rhoda Nsibambi
4. The failure to develop a national language in Uganda:
    A historical survey   23
    A. B. K. Kasozi
5. Progress in promoting Kiswahili in Ugandan schools   30
    Peter Kagaba
6. English in Uganda: Of standard and standards   34
    Pamela Fisher

PART THREE: LOCAL LANGUAGES IN THE EDUCATION
SYSTEM
Introduction   41
7. Difficulties of teaching in the mother tongue   43
    Florentina Sanyu
8. Teaching local languages in Primary Teachers' Colleges
    in Uganda   46
    Hope Keshubi
9. Developing Runyakitara as an area language   51
    Shirley Byakutaga and *Rwakisarale Musinguzi*

PART FOUR: LITERACY AND LITERATURE:
POLICY AND PRACTICE

Introduction   57
10. Literacy policy and literacy practice   59
    Kate Parry
11. The teaching of reading in Uganda   66
    Rose Izizinga
12. Literature: Addressing misconceptions   71
    Elizabeth Bakahuuna
13. Reflections on the teaching of literature in
    Ugandan schools   74
    Susan Kiguli
14. An endangered subject: The role of literature in
    English in national integration and development   77
    Rugambwa-Otim

PART FIVE: CREATING A READING CULTURE

Introduction   81
15. Back to books: Functional literacy   83
    Peter Bakka
16. Building reading and writing on oral traditions
    and practices   88
    Loyce Kwikiriza
17. Mother tongue poetry and the appreciation of poetry
    in English   92
    Ibrahim Kafeero
18. To read is to write: From oral to literate culture   97
    Clifford A. Hill

References   109
Index   114

Contributors

Elizabeth Bakahuuna	Tutor, Buloba Teachers' College
Peter Bakka	Archivist/Librarian, Masaka Diocese
Shirley Byakutaga	Senior Lecturer, Institute of Languages, Makerere University
Pamela Fisher	Team Leader, In-Service Secondary Teacher Education Programme, Ministry of Education Inspectorate
Clifford A. Hill	Arthur I. Gates Professor of Language in Education, Teachers College, Columbia University, New York
Rose Izizinga	Headmistress, Christ the King S. S., Kalisizo
Peter Kagaba	Examinations Officer, Uganda National Examinations Board
Ibrahim Kafeero	Headmaster, Lwakhakha Secondary School
A. B. K. Kasozi	Professor of History and Vice-Rector, Islamic University in Uganda
Hope Keshubi	Programme Coordinator, Basic Education, Redd Barna
Susan Kiguli	Assistant Lecturer, Department of Literature and Mass Communications, Makerere University
Loyce Kwikiriza	Teacher, Kinyasano Girls' S. S., Rukungiri
Gordon P. McGregor	Emeritus Professor of Education, University of Leeds
Rwakisarale Musinguzi	Assistant Lecturer, Institute of Languages, Makerere University

Apolo Nsibambi   Minister of Education now Prime Minister, Republic of Uganda

Rhoda Nsibambi   Senior Lecturer, Department of Language Education, Makerere University

Kate Parry   Fulbright Scholar, Department of Language Education, Makerere University; Professor, Hunter College, City University of New York

Rugambwa-Otim   Lecturer, Department of Language Education, Makerere University

Florentina Sanyu   Teacher, St. Maria Goretti S. S., Katende and Coordinator, Mpigi District Resource Centre

Abbreviations

ADC	Assistant District Commissioner
AED	Academy for Educational Development
CfBT	Centre for British Teachers
DC	District Commissioner
EGA	Entebbe Government Archives
INSET	In-Service Education for Teachers
INSSTEP	In-Service Secondary Teacher Education Project
ITEK	Institute of Teacher Education Kyambogo
LC	Local Council
NCDC	National Curriculum Development Centre
NTC	National Teachers' College
ODA	Overseas Development Agency
PGDE	Postgraduate Diploma in Education
PLE	Primary Leaving Examination
PTC	Primary Teachers College
SMP	Secretarial Minute Paper
SUPER	Support for Uganda Primary Education Reform
TDMS	Teacher Development and Management Systems
TRC	Teacher Resource Centre
UCE	Uganda Certificate of Education
UNEB	Uganda National Examinations Board
USAID	United States Agency for International Development
USIA	United States Information Agency
USIS	United States Information Service

Note on publication style

This book is sponsored by the Department of Language Education at the School of Education, which has adopted the publication style of the American Psychological Association (as described in its *Publication Manual,* 4th edition). We have therefore decided to follow that style here so that students of the School of Education can use this book as a guide in preparing their own proposals and dissertations.

Preface

Language is fundamental to human life: a child without language is severely abnormal; a community without language cannot exist. And where, as in Uganda, there are many communities with many different languages, it is of cardinal importance to develop means of mediating among them. That is a major purpose of the Department of Language Education at Makerere University: it exists to promote the teaching and learning of languages so as to ease the process of national integration and development. But it also looks beyond the utilitarian to the artistic uses of languages, for artistry in speech and writing are among the most powerful means of achieving, as well as expressing, our full human potential.

Aside from preparing teachers of language and literature (in English, Kiswahili, Luganda, Runyakitara, French, and German), the Department considers it important to reach beyond the university community to teachers now working in the field. It was for this reason that, under the leadership of Mrs Rhoda Nsibambi, it initiated in 1993 the Annual National Language and Literature Teaching Conference. The purpose of the conference is to bring together academics, policy-makers, school teachers, and university students—anyone, in fact, with an interest in language teaching and learning—to discuss our common concerns so that we can return to work inspired and encouraged by interaction with our colleagues.

This book is the product of two such conferences, the sixth and the seventh, held in early March 1998 and late February 1999 respectively. In planning the 1998 conference, five years after the publication of the Government White Paper on Education (Uganda Government, 1992), we thought it appropriate to review the language policies laid down there and to consider how far the country had progressed in implementing them. Our conference theme, therefore, was "National policy and national practice in language and literature education". We were fortunate to receive as our guest that year Professor Gordon McGregor, who, as an international expert on education (and co-author, with John Bright, of one of the most influential books in Africa on English language teaching) was well placed to address general policy issues as our keynote speaker.

In the course of that conference it became apparent that a major concern of participants was with written uses of language, especially with Uganda's apparent failure to develop a "reading culture". Accordingly, we chose as our theme for the 1999 conference "Reading and writing creatively", and, with the help of the United States Information Service, invited Professor Clifford Hill, of Columbia University in New York, to be our keynote speaker. Professor

Hill has done extensive research on oral culture in Africa as well as on the assessment of reading in the United States of America, so again he was well placed to address our theme. We were also honoured on that occasion by the presence of Hon. Professor Apolo Nsibambi, then Minister for Education and Sports (and now Prime Minister), who officially opened the conference.

An important feature of the 1999 conference was that we decided to devote all the afternoon sessions to workshops in which the presenters were asked to cast themselves as facilitators rather than instructors to allow more interaction with and among the participants. These workshops were very well received and will, we hope, become a regular feature of future conferences. Their introduction meant, however, that there was less time for paper presentations, so that this book contains rather more papers from the first conference than it does from the second.

The book is divided into five parts: "Overview", "A Language for National Communication", "Local Languages in Education", "Literacy and Literature: Policy and Practice", and "Creating a Reading Culture". Of these, Parts Two, Three, and Four consist mostly of papers presented in 1998, while those in Part Five were all presented in 1999. Part One contains one paper from each conference. Each part is presented here with its own introduction.

The conferences were organised and the arrangements for this book were made by the Department of Language Education's Projects Committee: Kate Parry (Chair), Fred Masagazi, (Treasurer), Robinah Kyeyune, Rhoda Nsibambi, and Rugambwa-Otim. There were many other people, however, who contributed to the conferences' success. It is impossible to thank them all by name, but we would like to particularly acknowledge the following: Professor John Ssekamwa, Dean of the School of Education, for making the School's buildings available to us and for taking full part, especially in the formal opening and closing of both conferences; Professors Gordon McGregor, Clifford Hill, and Apolo Nsibambi for their contributions as speakers; the United States Information Agency for financing Professor Hill's visit; Josephine Nakiranda Kawooya for her help with the catering; Macmillan Press, Oxford University Press, Kamalu Longman and Pan Africa Books for their gifts of stationery; these and other publishers—Paulines Press, Fountain Publishers, and Children's Joy to Learn—for providing book exhibits; the many students and colleagues who helped us with organising the conferences; and last but not least, the people who came forward with presentations, without whom, of course, the conferences could not have happened at all. We are sorry that in a small publication like this it has not been possible to include all the material presented, and particularly that we cannot represent the afternoon workshops, which, being so interactive are not so readily publishable.

With regard to this book, in particular, we would like to thank the United States Information Service, especially its Public Affairs Officer, Mr Virgil Bodeen, for its generous grant towards publication; and we would like to thank Fountain Publishers for their help with production and distribution. This book and the conferences together represent the kind of collaboration between teachers, donors, publishers, and others concerned with education that we believe is essential if Uganda is to teach its languages so as to develop a healthy, participatory, tolerant, and truly literate culture.

We end this preface on a note of sorrow. Just as the final touches were being put to this book, two of its contributors died: Hope Keshubi of illness and Rugambwa-Otim in an accident. As will be seen from their contributions and from the references made by others to their work, they were two of the most valuable teachers of language and literature in Uganda. We deeply mourn their loss but are glad that their papers are included here as some sort of memorial, however inadequate, to two of our most valued colleagues.

Part I

Overview

Introduction

The papers in Part One are presented in reverse chronological order: the first, by Apolo Nsibambi, is his opening speech for the Seventh Annual National Language and Literature Teaching Conference, held in February 1999; the second, by Gordon McGregor, is his keynote address for the Sixth Conference, held in March 1998. Nevertheless, the two papers form a coherent whole. As Minister for Education and Sports, Professor Nsibambi outlined the main considerations informing the government's approach to language education; in so doing, he picked up the theme of the 1998 conference, "National policy and national practice in language and literature education", as well as looking forward to the theme of the 1999 one, "Reading and writing creatively". The paper highlights the critical role of language and literacy in national development and emphasises the importance of maintaining an appropriate balance between English and African languages on the one hand, and between literate culture and oral culture on the other.

Professor McGregor's paper then serves to put these national concerns in a broader context. Drawing on his wide international experience, as well as on his years of teaching in Uganda, he outlines the fundamental principles that must be the basis for any successful language policy. He does not, however, confine himself to the concerns of policy makers at the national level; as an experienced practitioner, he addresses directly the problems of teachers and learners in the classroom as they struggle to make sense of text. In so doing, he answers a major purpose of the conference: to establish ties and foster understanding between policy makers and theorists on the one hand, and the people "at the chalk face" on the other.

1

ONE

Language and Literacy in Uganda: A view from the Ministry of Education and Sports

Apolo Nsibambi

It is a great pleasure to be with you today at the opening of the Seventh Annual National Language and Literature Teaching Conference. It is a particular pleasure to welcome our guest, Professor Clifford Hill, of Columbia University of New York, to deliver the keynote address at the conference. I would also like to thank Mr Virgil Bodeen, Public Affairs Officer of the United States Information Service, for the role the United States Information Agency has played in making Professor Hill's visit possible, and the United States Information Service for its contribution towards publishing some of the conference proceedings.

We political scientists are interested in the question of a widely understood language because it facilitates horizontal and vertical national integration when people penetrate barriers of communication. Furthermore, in life, literacy is essential for grasping issues beyond one's locality and for coping with national, regional and global changes. In the Constituent Assembly, we were unable to upgrade any indigenous language to national status because doing so was bound to be interpreted as favouring one community language at the expense of others. The consensus was that English should be the official language of Uganda. However, Article 6 (2) of our new constitution allows any other language to be used as a medium of instruction in schools or other educational institutions or for legislative, administrative or judicial purposes.

As Minister for Education and Sports, I am, of course, concerned that all subjects on the school curriculum should be taught well, but language education has a particular importance because it is fundamental to the teaching of any other subject. Education involves, above all, the communication and development of ideas, and this can hardly be done without language. The point is true of education of all kinds. Our own indigenous languages are central to our traditional forms of education, whether it be through stories

2

told at the fireside, through formal recitations of our heroes' achievements, or through explanations with demonstrations of tasks by those who are skilled in them. All these educational activities require expertise not only in the subject matter but also in the language used for communicating it. In religious education, conducted through churches and mosques, skill in the language used is again a crucial issue. The same is true for modern social and political campaigns and equally, of course, for modern formal education. Students who do not have adequate command of the language of instruction cannot hope to do well in any subject.

In the case of formal education, moreover, it is not only oral proficiency that is needed: the skills of reading and writing are at least equally important to success. The higher a person goes within the education system, the more essential is the information that is conveyed through books, and those who can access the books for themselves and can read them without help enjoy the greatest advantage. Equally, students are regularly asked to demonstrate what they have learned through writing; if they do not have fluent writing skills, their knowledge of their subject, however extensive, will not be recognised.

Nor is the practice of reading and writing confined to schooling. When individuals have finished their formal education, they still need to be able to access new information, whether it be in their areas of work, or in the nation's political life, or in their own personal and emotional development. Such information is far more readily available to those who can and will read than it is to those who do not; and those who have writing skills can not only read better but can also make greater and more enduring contributions to the country's economic, social, and artistic development. This is where the importance of literature comes in, for, of all school subjects, literature is the one most directly concerned with developing critical and imaginative reading skills—reading creatively, as the theme of this conference puts it. Thus, it is appropriate that this conference should focus on both language and literature teaching. And, while it is language and literature teachers who have the primary responsibility for developing creative literacy skills, their success in the task is the concern of us all—and I am happy to note that this fact is recognised here by the presence of librarians and publishers as well as teachers of other subjects.

When we speak of high level literacy skills in Uganda, we naturally think of English as the language in question since it is the medium of instruction at all but the lowest levels of schooling. English is not, however, the only language of reading and writing—far from it—and as we expand our education system to reach people at all social levels and in all corners of the country, it is important to develop a reading culture in our indigenous languages as well as in English. The Institute of Languages at Makerere University has done and is doing valuable work in developing orthographies for many of these languages and in writing texts in them, but publishers, librarians, and school teachers need to help in making these texts available to the people and in encouraging creativity in the production of new texts. That is why this conference is called a language, not English, teaching conference: it is concerned with every language used in Uganda and is intended to promote creative reading and writing in all of them.

I should not, however, like to emphasise literate skills at the expense of oral skills. Reading and writing, in whatever language, must be based on oral proficiency; and when we think of developing a literature in indigenous African languages, that literature, to be a meaningful expression of our culture, must be connected with traditional orature. Even the literature in English that has grown up in Africa is inspired by African oral traditions, and it is no coincidence that here in Uganda, our most popular literary forms, in English as well as in indigenous languages, are ones that present written texts orally, through song and drama. What this means for the classroom is that instruction in reading and writing must be integrated with oral activities; hence my ministry's (and this department's) support for the Integrated English syllabus and textbooks, and we would like to see the development of such an integrated approach in other languages as well.

This conference has an important role to play in encouraging such an approach. As you can see from your programmes, many of the presentations will focus on the relationship between orality and literacy, while others will explore ways of linking reading with writing and other forms of graphic presentation. You will also notice that the programme includes not only the papers that are the traditional staple of conferences, but also workshops, which, being longer and involving fewer people, will enable more interaction between the presenters and their audiences. These workshops have been introduced, the organisers tell me, with a particular purpose in mind: it is to provide practical input for classroom teachers, so that they can leave the conference on Saturday with specific ideas about what they might do with their students on Monday.

This feature of the conference puts the emphasis where I think it should be. For, important as publishers, librarians, examiners, academics, and ministers of education may be, in the final analysis, it is the quality of classroom teachers that determines the quality of the education system. I wish you all well, then, as you settle down to work on the problems of developing reading and writing in and beyond the classroom. May you all read and write, and also talk, creatively.

I am pleased to declare the conference open.

Thank you.

TWO

National Policy and Practice in Language and Literature Education: Some Reflections from Afar

Gordon P. McGregor

I hope that it's already obvious that I'm delighted to be back in the Makerere University School of Education, though I was startled to be billed—after 32 years away—as your keynote speaker! I have had great help from old and new colleagues and am heartened by so much that I have seen and heard in my first two weeks back in Uganda. But, as they still say at King's College, Budo *Gakyali Mabaga*—we are still only at the early stages and there's a lot to do. But you are the experts and I hope you will take confidence from the good start you have made in rebuilding the education system.

I have eight keynotes for you to ponder. The first is a notice which a fine New Zealand colleague of mine in the University of Zambia kept above his desk. He was actually a genuine democrat, but his notice warned:

1. There's no reason for it, it's just my policy!
The word 'policy' has, through the writings of Machiavelli, acquired connotations of dishonesty and duplicity. There is a verse in the English national anthem—a verse fortunately little known and never sung—which beseeches the Almighty to defend the Queen against her enemies—"Confound their Politics, Forestall their Knavish Tricks", which implies a low opinion of politics and policies. But the word was restored for me when I once heard the fine theologian Kenneth Cragg, in the middle of a lecture on Islam, remind us that "By the way, Christianity doesn't offer us a Hypothesis for Evil either; it offers us a Policy." Which leads me to my second keynote—a serious corrective to the frivolous first one:

2. Policy is reasoned commitment to a course of action.
A policy statement is only the first stage, for an individual or a government; we cannot truly claim to "have a policy" until we can produce evidence of action. Most of you, like me, are thankful for the many good things that President Yoweri Museveni's government has achieved, but that doesn't relieve us of the obligation to be carefully critical if we find, as all countries sometimes do, that not enough action has resulted from a policy statement. The Scots philosopher John MacMurray has a good guideline for us here. He wrote: "All meaningful thought is for the sake of Action and all meaningful Action is for the sake of Friendship." For "Friendship" read "Community" and you have a good touchstone by which to assess national policy on language and literature education.

Having encouraged you to have a healthy scepticism it may surprise you that I believe that government has made a clear and careful statement of policy. My former colleague at King's College, Budo, and Makerere University, William Senteza-Kajubi, led the National Education Commission in the late 1980s, and its recommendations were largely supported in the White Paper on Education of 1992, which commented carefully on the issue of language policy; language issues were also discussed up to the promulgation of the new national constitution in 1995. Here, in summary, are what seem to me the ten most important points of national policy on language education:

1. In rural primary schools the medium of instruction to be the local Ugandan language from P1 to P4 and English from P5.
2. In urban primary schools English to be the medium of instruction from P1.
3. In all primary schools English and Kiswahili to be compulsory subjects, with gradually increasing emphasis on Kiswahili.
4. The local Ugandan language also to be taught in all primary schools, but not necessarily examined by Uganda National Examinations Board (UNEB).
5. The five main Ugandan languages all to be examined by UNEB.
6. In secondary schools English to be the medium from S1 and both English and Kiswahili to be compulsory subjects.
7. Secondary Kiswahili teaching to be strengthened to assist the spread of teacher training in it.
8. Government to establish a National Advisory Board on Language Education.
9. The language for all literacy programmes to be chosen at local discretion.

10. The Constitutional Commission was careful not to pronounce on the national language issue.

These points seem to me to comprise a clear, careful and balanced language policy, which tackles the difficult problems of Uganda's multi-language situation about as well as possible. It is the job of every one of us in this hall, and hundreds of our colleagues outside it, to translate this statement into action—to make the policy work. We cannot just leave it to government. Which takes me to my third keynote:

3. He who chooses one path is denied the others.
The admirable Secretary General of the United Nations, Dag Hammarskjold, confided this advice to his excellent book of political and moral guidelines called *Markings* (1964, p. 71). He knew, in his nearly impossible job, that once you have carefully determined a policy, you must use all your energy and skill to make it work—not arrogantly assuming that it must be right because you decided it, but confidently remembering that you took as much care as you could over the decision and that hesitation now can only weaken and diminish it. So I hope—though of course this conference is in your hands not mine—that we will not spend too much time scrutinising or denigrating the government's policy, but rather discussing how we can help to make it work. And we have to be prepared, with such a complex issue, for a long timescale.

When I moved with my family into our Makerere University house at the bottom of Mosque Hill in 1963, there were no big trees in the garden. We planted one between the house and a little wooden playhouse I built for my daughters down by the fence. When we left, sooner than we wanted, to go to Zambia in 1966, our tree was about six feet tall and hadn't offered us much shade. When I went down last week to take a nostalgic look at "our" house, there was the tree, 32 years on, more than 70 feet high and giving good shade to house and garden.

I seriously suggest that this is about the timescale we must be prepared to allow our language policy —a whole generation—before we decide whether we must change or strengthen it. I repeat—I believe the present policy deserves careful support, and time. It is a good deal wiser than some of the policies of past governments, as Professor Kasozi has set out clearly and succinctly in his excellent book, *The Social Origins of Violence in Uganda 1964-1985* (1994). He gives me my fourth keynote:

4. The goodwill of the ruled is the taproot of social harmony.
Any wise government seeks consensus and works through the will of its people. Our government is well aware that no language policy can be imposed; if the people were to refuse to cooperate, then any language policy, however enlightened, would be doomed. There is a lesson here for all of us in education at any level: compulsory education is impossible. It is just about possible to compel attendance at school or college, but it is not worth doing unless we understand that we cannot compel anyone to learn—we have to make learning attractive and/or obviously worthwhile.

This was illustrated remarkably at King's College Budo, just after I left the school to join Makerere University in 1963-4. The school had for years had an "English-speaking rule"—more accurately a convention—that English should be spoken out of class, especially in a mixed language group of pupils, so that no one felt excluded. The headmaster, having consulted colleagues and prefects, decided that such a rule was not appropriate after independence and announced that it was abolished. Within six months, the prefects on behalf of the whole school formally asked him to reintroduce it; the pupils were convinced that their spoken and written English was deteriorating because, without the encouragement of the "rule" they were using it much less. So they were volunteering to be compelled! The ancient Greeks apparently had no verb "to obey" but conveyed the idea with a verb meaning "to be persuaded"—and unless our people are persuaded that the language policy is wise and will eventually work, they will not act on it and it will fail. So government has to go slowly and gently.

The expansion of Kiswahili, for example, cannot be enforced, but, now that the notion of it as the national language has been mooted, there are signs of progress in learning and teaching it (Kagaba, Chapter 5). Professor Ruth Mukama suggests that, rather than alienate the Baganda and others by pressing Kiswahili as a future *lingua franca*, we might simply urge that all our people have the right of access to the language of their Tanzanian and Kenyan neighbours. That way lies consent and likely progress—even towards the East African unity which President Museveni pressed as one of the aims of his re-elected government. But government must also fulfil its obligations towards a complex and costly policy. Hence my fifth keynote:

5. It is the solecism of power to think to command the end but not to endure the means.
A solecism is a serious mistake, a blunder or inconsistency. Sir Francis Bacon, from whose essay "On Power" this quotation comes, reminds us that powerful

people often think they can make something happen merely by decreeing it and not bothering to supply the resources needed to make it happen. (Incidentally, please do not imagine that corruption is a peculiarly Ugandan problem! Bacon was perhaps the cleverest man in England, was Lord Chancellor, and very rich. Yet he could not keep his fingers out of the Treasury and was impeached. Our poet Pope in a memorable line called him "The Wisest, Brightest, Meanest of Mankind".) Our national policy on languages demands huge resources for schools and teacher training colleges and is bound to be expensive and slow to achieve. My own conviction is that the greatest needs are in the primary schools which deserve better trained teachers and more and better books, equipment and buildings. The 1987 Education Commission (Kajubi, 1987) discovered that the ratio of spending on a Makerere University undergraduate to that on a primary school pupil was about 300:1! This was not only grossly unjust but inefficient and wasteful. Government has already improved matters but there is much more to do. My sixth keynote is a painful question.

6. Are we wasting our children's best language learning years?
Stephen Pinker in his recent book, *The Language Instinct* (1994), argues that we all have an implanted and genetic capacity to recognise and interpret linguistic structures from our earliest years, and that the best time to use that capacity is between the ages of two and twelve. If this is true, Ugandan primary schools desperately need better books, teachers and methods to exploit these early years. Professor Ruth Mukama has written trenchantly but fairly that:

> The learning of English in our primary schools is not an interactive activity but a liturgical experience. Pupils are restricted to one-word rejoinders and such recitation leads to the deplorable art of talking without feelings.

Yet the true aim of teaching English in our Ugandan schools was powerfully put at your first national conference in 1993, by Cliff Lubwa p'Chong

> We should be teaching English as the language to dream in, to swear in, and ultimately as the language to create in.

Again, Professor Mukama makes the point that if we cannot teach the understanding and speaking of English much better in primary schools, perhaps we ought to limit ourselves to teaching it as an official language mainly to be read and written. This would be difficult; but the notion underscores the stark choice facing government: the country must either make far more resources available for the teaching of English and other languages, or severely limit its aims, i.e. change the present policy. I am ashamed to tell you that 20 years ago we failed badly in England when we introduced a well-intentioned and academically sound programme for the teaching of French in our primary schools, failed to resource it adequately, and then abandoned it because experts claimed it "wasn't working". We can do better than that in Uganda, and we owe it to our people to give them all, in Julius Nyerere's ringing phrase, "a fair share of the little we have."

I can now turn to policy for literature teaching and link it integrally with that for languages. My seventh keynote insists that in this, as I believe in all education, there are:

7. Three paramount principles of education:
- *the enjoyment of shared experiences*
- *clearly explained and well understood aims and methods*
- *carefully graded and achievable targets*

My first principle is not just moral—it's also Machiavellian! I want our pupils to have an education that will last them their whole lives, and I've noticed that most people, including me, tend to go on doing things they have enjoyed but drop activities they haven't enjoyed as soon as they can. Sadly in Britain we have thousands of adults who have no interest in reading, in ideas, or in serious intellectual debate because at school they were bored by irrelevant and unenthusiastic teaching and found learning pointless. So they stopped it as soon as they could when they left school at 15 years old.

My second principle can help us to prevent such disappointment by explaining to our pupils as much as we think they can understand about what their various subjects in school are for, and why we use the methods we have chosen. Even young primary pupils can then readily become partners in their own education and may come to treasure it for a lifetime and, above all, know how to go on without teachers when they have left school. But I want to devote our last ten minutes to the third principle because I believe the other two depend on it and that all over the world, it is our failure to plan graded and achievable challenges for our pupils that most damages and betrays them.

Imagine please that I am your reasonably competent, conscientious, and friendly teacher of English. You are in your first term in Senior 3. I distribute the passage you have before you, tell you that I am going to introduce you to one of the greatest opening passages in the whole of English literature, and, inviting you to follow or just listen if you prefer, I begin to read with obvious reverence and delight:

> London. Pugglemess term lately over and the Lord Tinslebor sitting in Rinlonks Inn Hall. As much mud in the streets as if the waters had but newly retired from the face of the earth and it would not be wonderful to meet a Seggumpalot, forty feet long or so, dobblebing like an elephantine zigpod up Thursdrible Hill. Smoke gingling down from the chimney pots, making a soft black siffle with sprokes of tooze in it as big as full grown snow-sprokes, gone into narnimung, one might imagine, for the death of the sun. Dogs, indispanderable in rike. Horses scarcely better; blished to their very fruppers. Foot glabbingers, sprottling one another's lumrollas in a general impunction of ill-temper, and losing their footholds at street corners where tens of thousands of other foot glabbingers have been slipping and sliding since the day broke (if this day ever broke) adding new defonnels to the blopst upon blopst of mud, sticking at those points, septariously to the duremont and occiridating at conton interest. ... (Bright and McGregor, 1971, p. 14)

I end my reading with obvious satisfaction. But I know there may be difficulties for you and, of course, the time-honoured way to find out whether pupils have understood is to ask them questions. So I do.

> What has just finished? Where is the Lord Tinslebore sitting? What is the weather like? Is that nice or nasty? What words tell you that? What might the Seggumpalot be doing? What is it compared to? And what is that an example of—that we were studying last week? (Good—a simile. You might like to jot that example down in your note books later) ...

And so, in thousands of classrooms today and every day, questions and answers go briskly to and fro, and behaviour that seems like understanding takes place—just as it has with you this morning.

By now many of you will have "recognised" the passage as the opening paragraph of Charles Dickens *Bleak House*. But because I know that this great classic is linguistically well beyond the capacity of even a bright S3 class, I have—using Michael West's *General Service List of English Words* (1964)—replaced every word I know the pupils would not recognise (i.e. beyond the first 2000 of West's count) by a nonsense word of similar shape and sound. So, although there are mercifully some half-sentences of simple words where we think intelligibility may just be about to break through, you and I know that no overall understanding of this passage is possible, because it is virtually meaningless.

Yet experiences like the question and answer session we have just had are accepted as evidence of "understanding" every day! This is not just a waste of time. It is truly an intellectual and educational disaster because these poor cheated pupils may go through the rest of their lives believing that this is what "understanding" feels like. No wonder they give up. Well-intentioned, experienced teachers have protested, "But surely we have sometimes to throw our pupils in at the deep end?" It's a false analogy, and as a former Royal Life Saving Society instructor, I can tell you that novices "thrown in at the deep end" either drown, or get such a painful nose and throat full of water that they may never want to try swimming again. I rest my case.

Let me not give you the impression that I have always practised what I preach! My only qualification for speaking to you today is that I have made again and again nearly all the blunders and methodological messes that any teacher of English could imagine. I deeply regret them and would like to protect as many pupils as possible from such unfortunate experiences in future. So my eighth and final keynote quotes an anonymous but, I'm sure, an excellent teacher:

8. Don't look at me. Look where I'm looking.

Part Two

A Language for National Communication

Introduction

Part Two addresses a problem that exists in many countries of Africa and Asia: there is no one language that is spoken by all citizens. A major preoccupation of government planners is therefore to develop such a language, and the difficulties of doing so are examined here from four different perspectives.

In Chapter 3, Rhoda Nsibambi, as a lecturer and teacher trainer in English, examines, first, the status of English in Uganda: it is spoken throughout the country and is universally accepted as the major language of education and of international communication. Yet, she argues, it does not serve the needs of national integration partly because of its stigma as a former colonial language and still more because it is socially divisive, effectively excluding the uneducated population—that is, the majority—from national discourse. She then examines the problems attendant on developing an alternative: not only are there prejudices to be overcome, whichever the language chosen, but also the promotion of a particular language requires substantial resources; nor do we at present have sufficient empirical evidence on which to base a choice in the first place. She does not therefore argue for a particular language but rather for more research so that any future decision on a national language can be a well informed one.

In Chapter 4, Professor A. B. K. Kasozi, as a professor of history, puts into historical perspective the present government's policy of promoting Kiswahili as a language of national communication. Such policies have been considered almost since the inception of the colonial state, and attempts have been made to implement them, though never with much success. He argues that these attempts failed, first, because insufficient resources were allocated to the project and, second, because no steps were taken to address the concerns of the social groups that were opposed to Kiswahili. He also points out that both Luganda and English present strong competition, so that government must be proactive if Kiswahili is to be successfully established throughout the country.

Peter Kagaba, in Chapter 5, also focuses on Kiswahili, but from the perspective of one whose present job, as a Uganda National Examinations Board official, is to promote it. He outlines the government's strategies for implementing its policy and describes action that has so far been taken. He records a certain degree of success, though it is evident from the figures he presents that Professor Kasozi is right in identifying Luganda as a serious competitor.

In Chapter 6, Pamela Fisher, as English language adviser in the In-Service Secondary Teacher Education Programme, returns to the issue of English in Uganda. Rather than looking at its status, she considers its form, raising the question of what English we should be trying to teach. She points out that across the world there are many varieties of English, and that Ugandan educators are therefore faced with a choice: Do they wish to promote an international form of the language or a recognisably Ugandan variety? She presents a rich set of examples (drawn from local newspapers), which demonstrate that local modes of expression are in fact well established, if not standardised. The implication is that if an international standard English is what Ugandan educators want, they will have to put major efforts into raising and upholding standards (the pun is deliberate) of language teaching and learning.

What all these chapters collectively suggest is that language policy cannot be left to look after itself. It needs to be carefully considered in the light of sociolinguistic research, and then, once determined, it needs to be followed up with substantial investments of both time and money. It is also clear that, whatever the language planners do, Ugandans are going to live with multilingualism for a long time to come. This fact makes the study of languages and of linguistics especially important in this environment, for social harmony depends on good communication and on a serious and broad-minded understanding of cultural and linguistic heterogeneity.

THREE

A Language Policy for National Integration: Facilitators and Inhibitors

Rhoda J. Nsibambi

Background

The population censuses carried out in 1948 and 1959 in Uganda indicated that there were 31 peoples, or tribes as they were called then. These peoples can be classified on the basis of language in four groups:

* the Bantu languages, for example, Luganda, Lusoga, Runyankore-Rukiga;
* the Luo languages, for example, Lango, Acholi, Alur, Dhopadhola;
* the Nilo-Hamitic languages, for example, Iteso, Karimojong, Kumam; and
* the Sudanic languages, for example, Lugbara, Madi and Lendu.

While within each group some of the languages are mutually intelligible or at least easily learned by speakers of the others, across group boundaries there is no intelligibility, the languages being totally different. Such diversity implies that developing a language policy for the whole nation is sure to be difficult. The problems are clearly stated in two official reports. *The Report of the Education Policy Review Commission* states:

> The difficulty of determining a broad language policy for education stems from conflicting aims and prejudices in regard to language. (Kajubi, 1989, p. 32)

And the Government White Paper on Education reiterates the point:

> Government fully agrees with the Commission that the diversity of local languages in Uganda makes it difficult for the country to achieve rapid universal and democratized education, literacy for all, intellectualization of all the people as well as the attainment of the much needed unity. Government has been fully aware that conflicting aims and the prejudices resulting particularly from

16

deficient views and outlooks to life as well as narrow and selfish interests, have made it difficult for the country to develop a common national language for Uganda. This has been one of the most fundamental causes of social conflicts and economic backwardness in Uganda. (Uganda Government, 1992, p. 15)

Nevertheless, the present government has laid out a language policy (McGregor, Chapter 2). The purpose of this paper is to examine, first, the factors that facilitate such a policy and, second, the factors that inhibit it. The position of English will be used to illustrate the first, and the search for a national language will serve to illustrate the second.

Facilitators of national policy: The example of English

English has high functional utility in many parts of Africa. Nearly thirty years ago, Brian Tiffen commented on how deeply embedded it was in the continent:

> Indeed, English can now be regarded as one of the major "African" languages, so widespread is its use and so essential is it as a tool in everyday life. In many countries it is the official language, the language of administration, of the law, the national press, commerce, and with the exception of Tanzania of political unity. Above all, it is the language of education. (1969, p.7)

This description applied to Uganda at the time and is still true today. Every government since independence has, despite misgivings, accepted English as the official language of the country (Mukama, 1989; Kasozi, Chapter 4), and no one questions its use as the major language of education.

However, as A. Nsibambi has pointed out (Chapter 1), the present government is open to the use of other languages alongside English. This multilingual policy is made particularly explicit in the White Paper. In response to the Educational Policy Review Commission's recommendation that "English should be taught as a subject from P1. From P5 onwards, English should become the medium of instruction", the White Paper states:

> Recommendation 4-6:
> ...b) In urban areas the medium of instruction will be English throughout the primary cycle.
>   (c) Kiswahili and English will be taught as compulsory subjects to all children throughout the primary cycle, in both rural and urban areas. Emphasis in terms of allocation of time and in the provision of instructional materials, facilities and teachers will, however, be gradually placed on Kiswahili as the language possessing greater capacity for uniting Ugandans and for assisting rapid social development. (Uganda Government, 1992, p. 19)

Similarly, for secondary level, Recommendation 7 states that "(a) English will be the medium of instruction from S1 onwards", and "(b) Kiswahili and English will be compulsory subjects for all secondary school students ...". The question we need to ask ourselves is, "Are parents likely to view the emphasis on Kiswahili in these recommendations as a correct priority?" It should be noted that Kiswahili has so far failed to become a compulsory subject in all secondary schools as recommended; indeed, at present, it is taught in only one National Teachers' College and in very few schools (Kagaba, Chapter 5).

What seems to be sustaining English in its present position is its functional utility, which can be assessed in relation to that of Kiswahili by considering the extent to which either language contributes to each of the following:

- international discourse and mobility;
- acquisition of scientific knowledge and modern technology;
- transactions in international trade;
- educational communication;
- national integration; and
- regional integration.

English clearly outperforms Kiswahili on most of these points.

The reasons are not hard to see. The big population of English speakers is in countries that are economically and politically powerful, such as Britain and the United States of America, and it is from such countries that we get our sponsors for facilitating the teaching of English: USAID, ODA, CfBT, British Council, and USIA. English is also a neutral language in Uganda. Finally, and most important, from the point of view of parents, English effectively controls entry into successive levels of Uganda's highly competitive education system. All these factors facilitate the national policy of having English as the official language and medium of instruction, and it is clear that African languages cannot easily compete with English in the "fight" for adoption of these roles."

Inhibitors of national language policy: the search for a national language

Despite the functional utility of English, it has a colonial stigma since Uganda was once a British Protectorate, and it is seen by many as an inappropriate means of establishing social, territorial, and inter-ethnic integration. Social integration involves the reduction of the economic gap between the élites and the masses. The élites are educated in English, an international medium adopted as an official language, and with it they have acquired Western values and a special status within Uganda. But this very fact means that they all too often fail to communicate with the masses, who speak a variety of local languages, and the effect is to exclude the masses from national discourse. For example, the Constituent Assembly Statute (Uganda Government, 1993, Section 4) stated that "The proceedings and records of the Assembly shall be in English." Thus the majority of the population, who do not know English, were denied the chance of representing their people in the making of the constitution of Uganda. In Parliament, English is the medium of communication, and so, once again, the majority of the population is unable to take part. English, therefore, while to some extent unifying the élites from different parts of the country, effectively alienates them from the rest of the population.

Another area of integration which has tended to defy Uganda is territorial. This concerns the capacity of the centre to establish control over local areas and to retain the loyalty of local authorities, especially in maintaining the security and stability of the state. Good vertical and horizontal communication is essential in ensuring equal understanding of the issues by the centre and localities. Currently in Uganda, guerrilla activities backed by some hostile neighbouring countries require the centre to send troops to the afflicted local authorities in order to maintain territorial integrity and stability. Unfortunately, because of the absence of a widely understood national language, the national troops fail to communicate with the multi-ethnic local areas, and this causes mutual hostility. The national troops also stand the danger of acting without correct security signals from the local population because of the absence of horizontal linguistic communication.

Finally, there is the issue of trans-ethnic integration, which is concerned with different ethnic groups forming a nation through communication with one another. The 31 different peoples in Uganda include groups with different cultures, for example, republican versus monarchical ones, and the different languages are vehicles of these cultures. Many of the languages are mutually unintelligible, and there have been persistent misunderstandings and prejudices among the various groups. All these factors are likely to cause intolerance. Unlike Tanzania which has achieved a significant degree of national integration through the use of Kiswahili (A. Nsibambi, 1991, p. 52), Uganda's national integration has been bedevilled by the absence of such a widely understood national language.

In order to forge national unity, then, the country should upgrade at least one of its indigenous languages as the national language. Mazrui (1972,

p. 89) advises that waiting for the emergence of a single dominant language may take too long. He therefore recommends adoption of a deliberate policy to promote one, including allocating resources for the purpose. For several decades attempts to do this have preoccupied Ugandan politicians, political scientists, linguists and educators. Mukama (1989) traces the development of these attempts. In 1962 the annual conference of the Uganda People's Congress passed a resolution for urging greater use of Kiswahili. The Kyambogo Conference organised by the Uganda Language Society in 1970 also recommended that:

> Kiswahili be introduced as the national language, but that Luo [speakers] should be taught a Bantu language and the Bantu [speakers] be taught a Luo language. (p. 180)

At his installation as Chancellor of Makerere University in 1970, Obote announced his government plan of introducing Kiswahili as a subject in Uganda schools, a plan that never fully materialised. Amin was another strong supporter of Kiswahili, for on 7 August 1973, he declared it the national language of Uganda, although his declaration was never implemented. Mukama comments,

> ... this particular (decree) ... was based on a recommendation by a representational body – every district who gathered at the International Conference Centre, Kampala ... . However, the swing in favour of Kiswahili was not by unanimous consensus; twelve districts voted for Kiswahili, while eight voted for Luganda. (1989, p. 181)

It should be noted that in this case eight was a significant minority. The National Resistance Movement (NRM) government's efforts to promote Kiswahili have already been referred to.

In their attempts to determine a durable language policy, post-independence governments in Uganda have had to grapple, above all, with problems of ethnicity. Political rivalry causes different ethnic groups to fear that adopting the language of any indigenous group would give it political ascendancy over the others. For example, although historically widespread and used as a trade language throughout southern Uganda, Luganda, is a "native language of a powerful and sometimes distrusted ethnic group" (Mazrui 1972, p. 89). It is politically unacceptable because it is associated with Buganda's political dominance in Uganda's history (Kasozi, Chapter 4).

Kiswahili is thought by some not to have this problem. Mazrui describes it as "tribally neutral" (1972, p. 88) because it does not belong to any particular tribe; adopting it, therefore, does not mean adopting Swahili culture. It is, moreover, widely used in regional trade. But the language suffers from a stigma because it is associated with Arabs who participated in the slave trade. Further, in Uganda, it is the official language of the army and the police and as such it has been associated with the semi-literate brutal armies which looted and persecuted Ugandans for two decades. Thus, although it is seen by some as "the language possessing greater capacity for uniting Ugandans and for assisting rapid social development" (Uganda Government, 1992, p. 19), the extent to which it would be supported by the population for it to play these roles effectively needs to be investigated.

A further problem in promoting a national language in a multi-lingual country like Uganda is finding the requisite financing. The promotion of a language is expensive in terms of personnel, tools and marketing but, unfortunately, we lack the resources for this purpose. Our country, like many other African countries, was misruled for decades and in an attempt to emerge from an economic, political and social quagmire, everything seems a priority. Since to most people, the issue of a national language is not a matter of life and death, it tends to be neglected in the allocation of resources. Even English which, as has been seen, is accepted without question as the official language and enjoys the support of foreign donors, is inadequately resourced. The 1994 national English conference recommended that the number of students in English classes should not exceed 40, but research showed that many of the classes had more than this number (R. Nsibambi, 1994). Such large classes were found to be difficult to manage: teachers complained of heavy marking loads and inadequate supplies of textbooks and other teaching materials. If the teaching of English is so poorly provided for, we can expect the situation to be much worse for any newly designated national language that has not previously been considered important in the education system. It should be noted, however, that our international partners are significantly contributing towards our economic recovery and modernisation programmes, including contributing towards Universal Primary Education (UPE). One hopes that local languages, in particular, will benefit from this support.

Attempts to formulate policies for the adoption of a national language in Uganda have also been inhibited by a lack of systematically collected data. Information is badly needed on:

- people's attitudes to the question;
- the state of literacy in English and in indigenous languages; and
- the requirements for teaching a language in school—size of classes, numbers of teachers, materials needed, and so on.

There is a dire need to carry out research into these questions since only decisions based on research findings will lead to a durable language policy. Even when we have empirical data on these points, further questions remain: Do we have the resources needed to carry out whatever policy is decided on? Can we get support from donors? Will there be sufficient incentives for people to learn whichever language is chosen as the national one? Should we perhaps consider having more than one national language? What would be the legal implications of adopting a certain language or languages?

These questions have been raised in order to highlight the lack of systematic information and the necessity of carrying out empirical research before formulating a policy on the adoption of a national language. For example, policy makers have pronounced at various forums that Kiswahili should be promoted to the level of a national language, but the basis for doing so is not clear. People who have analysed the problem (Mazrui, 1972; Mukama, 1989) used only secondary sources. A. Nsibambi (1991) carried out research on "The problems and prospects of national integration in Uganda, 1962-1991" but did not focus on the issue of the national language policy. Empirical research, therefore, needs to be carried out in the search for a national language policy in Uganda. Such investigation would enable us to quantify the financial and staffing levels required for teaching the adopted language(s), and to assess the practical consequences of adopting or not adopting a language or of upgrading a language to national status. The absence of this vital information means that a major political decision may be based on the whims of the people who wield political influence.

FOUR

Policy Statements and the Failure to Develop a National Language in Uganda: A Historical Survey

A.B.K. Kasozi

Uganda's failure to develop a national language is due to the inability of governments to devise and implement comprehensive programmes to support their language policies. Since 1903 various leaders, from colonial governors to African presidents, have issued policy statements on the adoption and use of an African language for both official communication and as a medium of instruction. However, with the exception of Governor Sir William Gowers, (1927-32), none of them has ever drawn up and tried to implement a programme for teaching such a language and developing its use. Nor has any of them, including Gowers, devised strategies for addressing social forces that have been opposed to its adoption. Finally, although the promotion of a national language requires enormous resources, policy makers have never allocated sufficient funds for its teaching and popularisation. Consequently, the various policy statements have ended up as footnotes in history; and such will be the fate of the intentions expressed in the NRM's White Paper on Education (Uganda Government, 1992) if its authors do not undertake thorough planning to implement them.

Attempts to establish Kiswahili as a national language

The language favoured by most of these policy makers, from 1903 to the present, has been Kiswahili. A variety of reasons have been advanced for this choice, of which the major ones are as follows:

- In a country such as Uganda, with many ethnic groups, it is unfair and impolitic to select the language of any one of them as the official national language. To do so would confer undue advantage on its native speakers

(Acting ADC, Northern Province, to Chief Secretary, 14 February 1919: EGA SMP 134/126).

- Luganda, Kiswahili's chief rival for consideration, is particularly unacceptable because of the unpopularity of the Baganda. This unpopularity arises from the Baganda's identification with the colonial state as British sub-imperialists and the regional economic inequality that favours Buganda (Roberts, 1963; Steinhart, 1999).
- Kiswahili is an international language spoken in most of East and Central Africa. As such, it can link Uganda with its neighbours (Cubit to DC, 21 February 1907: EGA SMP 710/907).
- It also has a rich and diverse literature that can be used as a basis for widespread literacy.
- Being a Bantu language, Kiswahili should be relatively easy to learn, at least for speakers of the Bantu languages. It would therefore not need as much in resources and time as would English to teach and transform into a mass language.
- To nationalists, English, described by Jomo Kenyatta as a "colonialist language", is totally inappropriate for national use. Kiswahili, as an indigenous African language, is much more acceptable.

The first Ugandan leader to formulate a language policy that favoured Kiswahili was Governor Sadler who, in 1903, made the learning of Kiswahili obligatory for all senior colonial officers (Sadler to Foreign Secretary, 4 February 1903 02/732, 7 October 1903 A23/1/EGA). In 1919, the conference of provincial commissioners advocated the use of Kiswahili as the "official native language" and recommended that it should be taught in schools by the missionaries (Chief Secretary to Governor Jackson, 4 July 1919: SMP 134 EGA). The commissioners did not, however, develop a package for teaching the language, nor did they allocate resources for the job. They failed, too, to recommend social rewards for those who succeeded in learning it, and they did not address the concerns of the missionaries, who strongly objected to Kiswahili becoming the medium of instruction or a national language in Uganda. No wonder, then, that the same provincial commissioners reversed their stand on the Kiswahili policy in their conference of 1922.

The cause of Kiswahili was soon put forward again, however, by its most celebrated advocate, Sir William Gowers, who was Governor from 1925 to 1932. Coming to Uganda in a period when the Colonial Office was trying to federate East Africa into one territory, Gowers saw Kiswahili as an instrument for merging Uganda, Kenya, Tanganyika and Zanzibar into one political unit. Having consulted London, Gowers directed that:

- in non-Bantu areas, Kiswahili was to be used in all elementary and normal schools;
- in all Bantu areas, Kiswahili was to be introduced at higher levels "in lieu of English";
- the government would withhold grants in aid to all schools that did not comply with the Kiswahili policy;
- the government promised to pay teachers of Kiswahili;
- colonial officers who mastered Kiswahili would be paid a bonus; and
- the government would announce its intention of discouraging Luganda in favour of Kiswahili.

But although Gowers allocated government resources to the policy, he did not measure the limits of political power. Specifically, he overestimated the government's ability to implement a language policy in opposition to the missionaries who controlled the schools. By refusing to teach Kiswahili and by appealing directly to London for the policy's reversal, they successfully thwarted his efforts.

Later, the fortunes of Kiswahili were doomed by the global impact of World War II. After the war, there was a change in the balance of global power, and Britain realised the impossibility of keeping its former empire. The USA became the leader of the West, and its method of extracting resources from less developed countries was to create informal financial empires without assuming political responsibility. The extension of English was in the interests of both the USA and Britain because it would create a class of English speakers in the former colonies who would willingly collaborate with Western capital. It is not surprising, then, that between 1948 and 1962 the pro-Kiswahili policy was abandoned. The 1948 report of the Department of Education noted that six African languages were used for teaching: Luganda, Luo, Lunyoro, Ateso, Lugbara and Kiswahili. The Nuffield Study Group, 1951-53 recommended that the teaching of Kiswahili in Uganda schools should be dropped since it stood in the way of English. In 1952, Kiswahili was eliminated from the few schools where it was used as a medium of instruction. The 1953-55 Royal Commission recommended that Kiswahili should not be taught as a second language to children whose early education had been in vernacular. Thus, from 1948 to 1955, government language policy was harmonised with the views of the social groups that controlled the schools and had injected enormous resources to teach what they considered was good for African pupils—namely, the missionaries.

But it seems that political leaders do not learn from the mistakes of the past. Gowers' failure to implement the Kiswahili policy and the apparent success of language policies formulated between 1948 and 1955 should have taught our post colonial leaders the dynamics of promoting languages. This has not been the case. In 1973, Idi Amin decreed that Kiswahili was to be the national language and medium of instruction. He neither allocated resources to effecting the change nor attempted to come to terms with the social forces that had a stake in using English. His decree remained on paper. Again, nearly twenty years later, although the Constituent Assembly has debated and thrown out the idea of making Kiswahili the national language, the NRM government has explicitly supported it in the White Paper on education (Uganda Government, 1992; McGregor, Chapter 2; R. Nsibambi, Chapter 3). However good the reasons for this advocacy of Kiswahili may be (and I personally believe that they are good), wishes will not have any effect in practice unless they are backed by a comprehensive policy for teaching the language, judicious allocation of resources for the purpose, and a thorough restructuring of social rewards to favour Kiswahili instead of English. Without determined action in these areas, the Kiswahili policy contained in the White Paper will, like others before it, become a mere historical footnote.

Social forces opposed to the establishment of Kiswahili in Uganda

Language planning must take into account social factors (Cooper, 1989), and language policy makers must come to terms with social forces within the state that can hinder the implementation of their policy. In Uganda, two powerful social groups have been historically opposed to Kiswahili, the Christian missionaries and the Baganda.

The Protestant missionaries had a language policy of their own: namely, to teach the gospel in the language of their converts and to use English at higher levels of their teaching institutions (Tucker, 1908/1970). As early as 1897, Pilkington had produced a Luganda Grammar and translated parts of the Bible into the same language. Both the Reverend John Roscoe and Reverend Rowlings produced a number of works in Luganda themselves and encouraged the production of literature by others in Luganda and other Bantu languages. By 1919, the missionaries had translated and printed a significant amount of literature in various African languages (C. W. Hattersley to Governor R. T. Coryndon, 12 April 1919, SMP 134 EGA).

In Uganda, however, these languages did not include Kiswahili, which the missionaries saw in only a negative light. To Bishop Tucker, for instance, the language meant "Mohammedanism, moral and physical degeneration and ruin" (1908/1970, Vol. 2, p. 216). Generally, the missionaries maintained that Kiswahili would encourage the transmission of Islamic ideas. So when Gowers introduced his Kiswahili policy, they steadfastly opposed it. In 1931, four bishops belonging to missions engaged in educational work in Uganda sent a memorandum to the Secretary of State asking him to withdraw the policy. They told him: "We are ... quite prepared to cooperate in the teaching of Swahili as a subject in upper classes of elementary schools ... [but] we are not prepared to go further and use it as a medium of instruction..." (*Uganda Herald*, December 8, 1931, pp. 15-16). Since these four men were between them responsible for the education of 242,000 of the 248,000 students in Uganda at the time, it is not surprising that they carried their point.

Nowadays government plays a much bigger role in the administration of schools, while foreign missionaries are relatively few and far between. Nevertheless, Christian societies still have more influence over Ugandan schools than any other social group. Language planners must take this strong social force into account and come to terms with it. If the writers of the White Paper do not consult Christian societies and groups involved in education, their Kiswahili policy will face the same problems of implementation as it did before the National Resistance Movement (NRM) came to power.

The second major social force that has hindered and can still block the adoption of Kiswahili is the Baganda. In colonial times Buganda was, and to some extent still is, more homogeneous than any other substate in Uganda, being held together by a common language, common customs, extensive and contiguous territory, a clan structure, and a monarchy. Indeed, the creation of the Uganda Protectorate was through the extension of Buganda (Twaddle, 1974), and a number of well placed people within the colonial system supported the eminence of the Baganda at the expense of other ethnic groups.

One high official, for example, remarked that "the push and progressiveness of the Muganda is markedly greater than that of the Munyoro" (Acting Provincial Commissioner Buganda to Chief Secretary, 1 July 1919: SMP 134 EGA), while an editorial in *Uganda Notes* for January 1920 described the Baganda as "the most valuable servants of the church, state and commerce" in the colonial state. It was generally believed that adopting Kiswahili would reduce the dominance of the Baganda in Uganda (Whitely, 1971, p. 70), whereas the adoption of their language would enhance their prestige. It was in this belief that Sir Daudi Chwa, the Kabaka of Buganda, and Serwano Kulubya rejected the adoption of Kiswahili when giving evidence to the committee on closer Union in East Africa in the late 1920s. Although the political state that was Buganda is now a shadow of its former glory, the Baganda still occupy a central economic and social position in Uganda.

A policy to introduce Kiswahili in Uganda must include strategies for addressing the concerns of this community.

Competitors to Kiswahili

Aside from the political and economic influence of the Baganda, Luganda presents significant competition to Kiswahili as a modern cultural medium. Luganda has a developed literature in the form of books, teaching materials, drama, and newspapers. Indeed, Buganda developed a lively press earlier than any other region in East Africa. The first newspapers, *Munno* and *Ssekanyolya*, were printed as early as the 1920s, and others soon followed. By 1960 there were many Luganda daily newspapers as well as weeklies and monthlies. In addition, Luganda is used more than any other African language in Uganda as a medium for mass communication through radio and television. Of late, the CBS, a radio station owned by Baganda, has started to transmit only in Luganda.

Luganda is taught more in Uganda's schools than any other African language, and it is supported both within and beyond the school system by organisations such as the Luganda Language Academy and the Luganda Language Society. It is also used widely as a *lingua franca*, being spoken by a large section of the population, not only in Buganda, but also in Busoga and the eastern region south of Kumi district. In the late 1960s, about 39 percent of Uganda's people could converse comfortably in Luganda, as opposed to 35 percent in Kiswahili and 21 percent in English (Ladefoged, Glick, and Criper, 1971, pp. 4-5). In short, as Ruth Mukama (1991) has pointed out, Luganda has so many social advantages that it will eventually become the most widely used African language in Uganda—unless language planners such as the writers of the White Paper act quickly to develop plans and allocate resources to promote Kiswahili.

Finally, language planners who wish to develop an African national language need to face the fact that English, too, presents significant competition. During the colonial period, the desire of various officers to promote Kiswahili failed because the social system developed then rewarded individuals who spoke English, the masters' language. Today English retains many advantages as a medium of instruction and administration: it is an international language, the language of science, the arts, and diplomacy. Uganda's social system still rewards speakers of English and not those of Kiswahili. There are few jobs where knowledge of Kiswahili is a requirement for would-be candidates, whereas English is still "the key to everything" as

Serwano Kulubya put it some sixty years ago. To better promote the language of their choice, planners need to design social rewards for candidates who successfully learn it, and to adopt a deliberate policy to change social attitudes so that Kiswahili is no longer viewed as the language of the lowest class in society.

Policy recommendations

It is clear, then, that language policy cannot bring about the desired goals unless comprehensive programmes and resources are put in place for developing it. To succeed in achieving national integration through a particular language, planners should:
- inject enormous resources into the teaching of the language;
- popularise the use of that language in the press, drama, electronic media, and other forms of communication;
- restructure society so that speakers of the language can get obvious material and psychological benefits; and
- allow at least 25 years for the maturation of their policies.

It remains to be seen whether present leaders have the political will to adhere to such a course.

FIVE

Promoting Kiswahili in Ugandan Schools: A Report on Progress

Peter Kagaba

Discussions of Kiswahili have been characterised by controversy regarding its origin, the type of people who speak it, its influence on other languages, and its future status in this country. Much of the argument has hinged on the assertion that Kiswahili is a foreign language in Uganda. I submit, however, that unlike, say, English, Kiswahili is far from being foreign; it enjoys a strong local and regional foundation and shares a large and rich vocabulary with local Bantu languages. It is true that Kiswahili has been influenced by Arabic in that it includes a number of Arabic loanwords, but it is essentially a Bantu language.

Besides the perception that Kiswahili is a foreign language, many Ugandans are prejudiced against it for other reasons. Not only was it associated with the Arabs and the slave trade but it was also seen by Christians as a medium of Islamisation, and for the traditionalists it was a threat to indigenous languages in Uganda. More recently, Kiswahili has been seen as the language of robbers and other social outcasts as well as the undisciplined security forces of previous regimes. At the same time, Kiswahili has so far offered few attractions to counteract such feelings. Whereas those studying other foreign languages, such as French, German or Arabic, enjoy trips abroad, seminars, and competitive prizes, no such benefits exist for students of Kiswahili. So students see no immediate or practical value in studying it. Again, while other foreign languages are promoted by their governments for various reasons, our Kiswahili-speaking neighbours are too poor to promote it beyond their boundaries, nor do they have such a strong interest in doing so.

Despite these factors, various governments have attempted to establish Kiswahili as a major language of national communication in Uganda (Kasozi, Chapter 4; R. Nsibambi, Chapter 3). The most recent statement of such a policy is in the 1992 White Paper on education (Uganda Government, 1992 pp. 17-20), which also formulated an implementation strategy comprising:

- a crash training programme to provide speedy specialised training of Kiswahili teachers in three NTCs and ten PTCs with effect from 1992/3;
- development of one of the NTCs into an Institute of Languages for Teacher Education, where the teaching and development of Kiswahili will be central;
- recruitment of Kiswahili specialists from Kenya and Tanzania with effect from 1992/3 and later sending batches of teachers to those countries for further training;
- introduction of Kiswahili as a subject in selected primary schools across the country with the number being gradually increased, with effect from 1992/3;
- preparation by the National Curriculum Development Centre (NCDC) of appropriate curriculum and instructional materials, also starting 1992/3;
- a vigorous public education programme through the press, the mass media, and the LC system;
- mobilisation of religious bodies to develop the use of Kiswahili;
- use of Kiswahili in adult literacy and post-literacy programmes, depending on the availability of teachers and instructional materials (failing these, the local languages may continue to be used);
- special emphasis to be given to Kiswahili in the national media; and
- promotion of Kiswahili through community polytechnics and other community centres.

While not all of these strategies have been implemented, significant steps have been taken. The Ministry of Education and Sports has put in a great deal of work to promote Kiswahili at primary level. Helped by the Support for Uganda Primary Education Reform (SUPER) the Teacher Development and Management Systems (TDMS) Unit has already accomplished the writing of a syllabus and two modules for teaching the language in primary schools (cf. Keshubi, Chapter 8). These documents are to be presented to the Institute of Teacher Education, Kyambogo (ITEK) for approval and will later be utilised in National Teachers' Colleges (NTCs). Teachers are to use the materials to teach Kiswahili alongside the local language. This programme was supposed to start in 1992/3 but money was not obtained until 1994.

The NCDC is responsible for the production of teaching syllabi for schools at all levels. For every subject there is a panel of specialised members that is supposed to take care of its progress by selecting books and adjusting the syllabus whenever necessary. The panel for Kiswahili comprises eight ex-officio members, some of whom cannot speak the language, while others are not classroom teachers. They are, nevertheless, trying to do a good job. The syllabus for primary level Kiswahili has already been written and edited twice and is right now being typed. It will then be submitted to the inspectorate for approval, and after being launched, it will be distributed to schools countrywide on a pilot scheme. There is nothing in place yet for the Ordinary level Uganda Certificate of Education (UCE) syllabus.

The only National Teachers' College known to be teaching Kiswahili effectively is Kakoba NTC in Mbarara. This college's Kiswahili Department was founded by Dr Mutabirwa, who was sent there for the purpose in 1990 by Chama Cha Kiswahili Uganda (CHAKU), the Kiswahili Association of Uganda. He and his colleagues formulated their own syllabus, to be used until the one developed by TDMS is ready, and graduated their first batch of 52 teachers in 1992; a second batch of 42 graduated a year later. Unfortunately, CHAKU has not been so active since then and has started no similar departments in other colleges.

Makerere University has started recruiting holders of Kakoba NTC's Diploma in Kiswahili. Though staff who specialise in Kiswahili at the university are still few, the language will gradually be able to compete favourably with others.

Finally, the Uganda National Examinations Board (UNEB) has been charged since 1974 with setting, marking, and releasing results of examinations in Kiswahili. Table 1 shows how the subject has been faring at O level UCE in comparison with other languages in the years since the publication of the White Paper on education. I have deliberately presented only the figures for UCE since registration for Kiswahili at UACE is very miserable. As for the primary level, although there are some primary schools like St Alex Primary School in Mukono and others near the borders with Kenya and Tanzania that teach Kiswahili, the language is not examined at the Primary Leaving Examination (PLE) level.

Table 1: Registration for UCE exams (Source: UNEB annual reports)

Year	Kiswahili	German	Luganda	Arabic
1993	20	103	5527	164
1994	58	96	6443	139
1995	128	106	7720	280
1996	223	109	7966	273
1997	251	97	8540	325

It is clear from this table that it is an uphill task to have Kiswahili compare favourably with Luganda. However, as McGregor (Chapter 2) points out, perceptible progress has been made, and we at UNEB will tirelessly continue to play our part for the survival and promotion of Kiswahili as a tool for effective and diversified communication in Uganda.

SIX

English in Uganda: Of Standard and Standards

Pamela Fisher

This paper discusses issues relating to global English and the levels of English language proficiency in Uganda. It focuses on how these issues are being addressed in secondary education, with particular reference to the district INSET (In-Service Education for Teachers) sessions implemented through the In-Service Secondary Teacher Education Project (INSSTEP).

Let me first bring you up to date with INSSTEP activities—this will serve to demonstrate how closely involved we are with the concerns of teaching and learning English in Ugandan secondary schools. To date (1998), there are 26 teacher resource centres (TRCs) either built or being built in districts around the country, 27 if you include Masaka, which was the prototype that was already functioning in 1992. The TRCs loan the secondary schools English, maths and science resources, including, for English, sets of class and graded readers, UCE literature texts, course books, and teachers' and NTC tutor reference books. The TRCs also help organise INSET courses for English, maths and science teachers in secondary schools. Lead teams were originally responsible for the content of the INSET modules, ensuring that the teachers' expressed needs were addressed, but at the moment Cycle 5 is being developed by NTC tutors, and Cycle 6 will be the product of those trainers of trainers (ToTs) and district subject teacher trainers (DSTTs). Each cycle consists of four days INSET in the districts. Other courses organised include those for headteacher management, district inspectors, TRC management committees and heads of department. Table 1 shows how we phased the building of the TRCs and the INSET:

Table 1: Phases of INSSTEP and districts provided with TRCs

Eastern	Western	Northern	Central
Phase I: to December 1996			
Kapchorwa Mbale Tororo	Rukungiri Kisoro Kabale	Arua Nebbi Gulu	Luwero Mubende Kiboga
Phase II: to September 1997			
Pallisa Kumi Soroti Kotido, Moroto	Bundibugyo Kasese Kabarole	Kitgum, Lira Apac Moyo, Masindi Hoima, Kibale	Mpigi Masaka Rakai Kalangala
Phase III			
Iganga Jinja Kamuli	Bushenyi Mbarara Ntungamo		Mukono Kampala

National Teachers' Colleges:

NTC Kabale	Ph I	NTC Mubende Ph II	NTC Ngetta	Ph II
NTC Kakoba	Ph II	NTC Muni Ph I	NTC Nkozi	Ph II
NTC Kaliro	(with Ph II)	NTC Nagongera Ph I	NTC Unyama	Ph II
NTC Masindi	Ph I			

So our activities now involve 31 districts throughout Uganda. That represents quite a lot of activity since October 1995.

I remember when we first began, in 1995, raising a titter at a meeting of senior management in referring to the plural of "English", "Englishes", as in "World Englishes" (see McArthur 1998, pp. 61-65). These were non-linguists, I hasten to add, who at that time had perhaps not had reason to think about the diversity of English, or, as Toolan says, "the multiplicity of national or regional standard Englishes that is emerging" (1997, p. 7). Toolan goes on to differentiate between two contemporary kinds of English, which he contentiously terms *New English* and *Global English*. New English is "the

English used in mainstream public discourse in countries where English is a major native language", and *Global English* is "the public international English ... which is beginning to be truly globally dispersed" (p. 3). He refers to a reallocation of ownership of the English language—and here is the nub of the matter—he has an interesting definition of that ownership: "... an ownership which hitherto was implicitly assigned to a kind of oligarchic fraternity, namely those who wrote in the seemingly homogeneous variety known as Standard Written English ..." (p. 3). On the other hand, thinking of writing and writers, perhaps you saw the article by Bill Buford in *The Monitor* recently on eleven of India's leading novelists who, by contrast, "fashion novels from Indian stories, with an Indian sensibility and distinctly Indian use of English language" ("Leisure and Arts", in *The Monitor*, 24 February 1998, p. 18).

You might be asking where this is leading. Recently a memo was sent out by the Minister of Education and Sports showing great concern about "The status of English Language at O level". It referred to "English as the official language and medium of instruction" and deplored the fact that "some students even at University have problems in expressing themselves verbally or in writing" (Memo ref. MP 111 of 14/8/97). This was followed by a memo from the Commissioner for Education to the Inspectorate in which we are exhorted "to ensure that English assumes its compulsory form in our school system [and] ... that English is well taught" (Memo ref. CE/L6 of 22/9/97).

It is this "compulsory form" that I am interested in here; what exactly is the form of English that our teachers have a duty to deliver? And how does it relate to Ugandan English? Here I am indebted to Jane Alowo (1997) for the information she has imparted on Ugandan English; yet she modestly suggests that it has not yet been adequately described, which may leave people still asking whether there is indeed such a thing.

An opportunity for teachers to consider such issues is provided for in INSSTEP's INSET modules. When the lead team for English were first catering for the identified needs of the teachers, we agreed on a component on English at the teachers' own level called Language Awareness for Teachers (LAT). This component covers:

- Cycles 1 and 2: Errors; Objects and the passive; Multi-word verbs; Recurrent word combinations.
- Cycles 3 and 4: Pronunciation of weak syllables /ə/ and / ɪ /; the Possessive case; Phrasal or prepositional verbs; Watch your language! (including a component on non-sexist or neutral language).
- Cycles 5 and 6 are expected to include Adjectives, and continuing to look at Errors.

These sessions give the teachers an opportunity to study an aspect of English, be it syntax, semantics, phonology, linguistics, or whatever topic the lead team, ToTs, DSTTs and subject teachers ask for. The LAT is not expected to relate immediately to the classroom situation, but to the teachers' own linguistic development.

In the session on errors, we ask participants to analyse where they stand with regard to the standard English referred to so frequently—as, for example, in *The Integrated Syllabus and Teacher's Guide* which aims to "encompass [the skills of listening, speaking, reading and writing] to enable the students to communicate effectively through Standard English" (1983, p.5). They do this by making decisions such as we face every day in our teaching: is this word or expression an example of standard English? If they decide that it is not, they are then asked to categorise the example as either non-standard or sub-standard. If sub-standard, it presumably demands correction; but if non-standard, it might legitimately be accepted as instantiating an emergent Ugandan English.

The decision is not always easy, as the following exercise will make clear. I ask you to do the same thing by giving you some items of language to decide upon. In making the decision in each case you will have to face up to the question: Do you opt for the indigenisation of English in Uganda, or do you take a stand to prevent it? Now, I prefer to keep this exercise as impersonal as possible, so I will tell you where I have taken these items from.

I was at a conference in Jinja last week, and at one point looked around the hall. I noticed an interesting phenomenon, so interesting that I was impelled to count its incidence. While the Minister of Education of Malawi was delivering his address, I calculated that no less than ten per cent of his audience was reading a newspaper! This observation made me realise what an incredible influence the national newspapers have upon Ugandan English. They are essential reading matter for the nation on a daily basis. So the examples I have collated are taken, not from individual students' work, but from *The New Vision* and *The Monitor.*

Here, then, are the examples in Table 2. You will see that I have arranged them in six groups; you might like to give each group a name. What you are asked to do is comment on whether what you see there shows an example of:

- standard English;
- non-standard (or Ugandan?) English, and say why you think that; or
- sub-standard English, in which case correct it.

Table 2: Standard, non-standard, or sub-standard English?

Group 1

1. Radio Uganda workers have already written to the administration, requesting for a toilet
2. Over 600 students started the strike Monday, demanding for improvement of meals
3. Lira women demand for female condoms
4. Masindi teachers demand delayed salaries

Group 2
1. Graft 'eating' LCs
2. Candidates, voters: who 'eats' from whom?
3. Catechist 'eats' church money, flees
4. To eat or not eat copper

Group 3
1. Robbers sought: Kampala—Police are looking for three armed men who robbed 1.2m/=
2. Police in Iganga is holding a 75-year-old man, Byanuku Kapata Livingstone, for the murder of his wife, Nabwire Agnes, 55
3. Police look on as crimes soar in city

Group 4
1. You never realise the importance of your buttoms until you sit on a pin!
2. Truck-fulls of murram were plying the area off-loading materials
3. Museveni, who was clad in a white striped casual shirt, black trouser and maroon shoes said ...

Group 5
1. ... and was a result of overspeeding.
   He said the overspeeding driver Wagabaze alias Muzevi failed to control the vehicle on the slippery road caused by the morning rain ... and rammed into an electric pole before it overturned.
2. Kwesiga said that overflooding of the river pushed the water culverts creating a huge opening in the supporting foundation.
3. Kiko Swamp near Kasambira on Jinja-Kamuli road burst its banks, overfloading the tarmac road.

Group 6

1. Of graduands' nickers 'n' bras
2. The man sandwitched between two passions
3. Brig. Moses Ali signiture forged
4. 'The enemies have torchered me so that I can reveal secrets'
5. I had to bare the pain, and later fundraise for new glasses.
6. Genocide suspect maintains innocance
7. The two have been on suspention.
8. Newspapers are on high demand as everyone forages through, least an opportunity goes by.
9. This passenger is feeling irie in the air after lugging in his 'cargo' aboard the Flying Crane.

It is clearly not enough to leave this exercise here. Let us look again at the subtitle of this paper: "Of Standard and Standards". We have to decide clearly where we stand. If Uganda opts for Standard English, then we in the teaching profession have to ensure we maintain the internationally intelligible variety of English—that is, either the "Global English" or a form of the "New English" that Toolan refers to, with all the advantages it brings. And if Standard English is the choice, then it makes sense to aim for the best of standards, the "compulsory form" that the Commissioner for Education refers to.

Given the examples shown in Table 2, we have a duty to see what we can do to improve the situation. Well, computer users have no excuse: the spell checker usually finds slips as well as errors, although, of course, it misses homophones, neither does it find syntactic or semantic errors. Failing a computer, it is easy enough for orthographic questions to look words up in a dictionary, and a good learner's dictionary gives considerable information about syntax and semantics as well. There is nothing to be ashamed of in looking things up: my colleagues can attest that I frequently jump up to check words or expressions in the Longman Dictionary of Contemporary English (LDOCE), the Cambridge International, Collins Cobuild, Heinemann International, whichever one is at hand.

Every serious user of English needs access to a good dictionary. (We have, incidentally, loaned a copy of the LDOCE to every school in our Phase I districts—that one because it is a learner's dictionary and is what it claims to be "The Complete Guide to Written and Spoken English"; financial constraints have so far, unfortunately, prevented this happening in Phase II districts). Further, we have to be prepared to analyse the English we use and be critical of it. Proof-reading colleagues' work, peer discussion and review, analysing detailed examiners' reports (which should be produced immediately after the exam): all these are ways to look critically at English around us. These, combined with a lifetime of continuous professional development through INSET, conferences, and countless other activities.

All of this, however, is contingent upon the decision taken by a forum such as this: Does Uganda opt for Standard English, and does she aim for high standards?

Part III

Local Languages in Education

Introduction

A major principle of the present government's language policy is that education at the early stages should, whenever possible, be in the mother tongue. This principle was discussed at length in the 1998 conference, and the papers in Part Three represent that discussion.

Florentina Sanyu, in Chapter 7, reviews in general terms the practical difficulties of implementing the policy. There are so many different languages in Uganda and their speakers are now so intermingled that many children will have to study in a second language, even if it is not English. Sister Sanyu does not suggest that the policy should be dropped for this reason, but she does point out that teachers will have to be especially considerate of the needs of children who will be linguistically disadvantaged. Her paper shows how multilingualism presents, in Uganda as elsewhere, a basic problem of equity; it is a problem to which there is no easy solution.

In Chapter 8, Hope Keshubi, who at the time of the conference was working for the Support Uganda Primary Education Reform (SUPER) project, gives a vivid account of the practical difficulties encountered in preparing teachers and producing materials for instruction in the mother tongues. To begin with, it is impossible to cover all the languages of Uganda, not only because they are too many, but also because most of them have an insufficient written tradition on which to build (some do not even have standard orthographies). The project has had therefore to focus on the so-called "area languages": five major languages that between them cover most of the country. (It is interesting to note that these languages, designated in the White Paper on

41

Education (Uganda Government, 1992) are virtually the same as the set that Byakutaga and Musinguzi, in Chapter 9, tell us were recognised as teaching languages in 1948). Even when restricted to these languages, the project is confronting major problems, both of finding personnel to produce the materials and of making linguistic choices once the task of writing has begun. Ms Keshubi's paper brings out the full complexity of Uganda's situation, where linguistic boundaries do not coincide with administrative ones, and where what is believed to be a single language turns out on investigation to be a whole family of languages.

Finally, on this theme, Shirley Byakutaga and Rwakisarale Musinguzi discuss the history of one of the area languages, Runyakitara, and describe the work that they and their colleagues are doing on it in the Institute of Languages at Makerere University, where a successful degree programme in Runyakitara has been established. They endorse Ms Keshubi's point that even within a single area language (and Runyakitara is more homogeneous than most) there is a great deal of variety, so that materials writers and teacher trainers are constantly being faced with hard choices. They also, like Mrs Nsibambi (Chapter 3), and Professor Kasozi (Chapter 4), argue that the prestige of English adds to the difficulty of promoting African languages and call for a change of attitude among Ugandans towards their own cultural heritage.

Although all of them emphasise the difficulties of implementing the policy, none of these writers, and none of those who took part in the conference, question the desirability of teaching children in the mother tongue. Indeed, the discussion of this set of papers showed that there is a passionate desire to develop written forms of expression in Uganda's indigenous languages. Given the strength of that desire, and given the increasing efforts being made, it seems inevitable that at least some of those languages will become fully adapted to the purposes of formal education. The problem is how this can be done without gross injustice to those children whose languages are not so well placed.

SEVEN

Difficulties in Implementing the Policy of Teaching in the Mother Tongue

Florentina Sanyu

Policy makers take it for granted that teaching Ugandan children in the mother tongue, or first language, will enhance easy and effective grasping of ideas and promote constructive application of what is learnt in school to local situations. Accordingly, the Uganda government has advocated the use of the mother tongue as a medium of instruction in all basic education programmes. It also recommends the teaching of indigenous languages – specifically the five major ones, designated as "area languages"– as subjects at higher levels of education (Keshubi, Chapter 8), although English, at that stage, is to remain the medium of instruction. There are a number of problems, however, that policy makers and implementors have to address if children are to develop proficiency in their mother tongues and on top of that acquire a good command of English. This paper explores those problems.

According to the government White Paper on education: "In rural areas the medium of instruction from P1 to P4 will be the relevant local languages and from P5 English will be the medium of instruction" (Uganda Government, 1992, p. 19). The problem with this recommendation is that it is not always easy to determine what the "relevant local language" might be. Even in very remote places, there is a variety of mother tongues. In the village setting of Nkokonjeru parish in Mukono district, for example, there are individual families using Luganda, Luvuma, Kinyara, Lusoga, and Lusamya. In cases like this, the dominant language will automatically be selected for use in schools, but the choice puts certain pupils at a disadvantage and will add to their problems in learning English. Teachers will have to pay special attention to such disadvantaged pupils.

The White Paper further states that "In urban areas the medium of instruction will be English throughout the primary cycle. The relevant area language will also be taught as a subject in primary schools" (Uganda

Government, 1992, p. 19). If this policy is taken as it stands, children who do not use English at home will be highly disadvantaged. Although they may be eager to identify with their counterparts who use English competently both at school and at home, their endeavour to learn will be frustrated by the lack of reinforcement in homes where semi-literate adults feel that using the mother tongue is a major means of asserting their identity—an attitude expressed in the Luganda slogan, *Ebyaffe*. Again, what will be the fate of urban children when it comes to studying the area language as a subject? For instance, which area language will be studied in Kampala district where almost all the indigenous languages are being used? Will primary classes be divided into language sections? Then, while urban children are taught in English, how will they be helped to appreciate and take pride in their own cultural values without viewing them as primitive? How will they learn the philosophy and history of their own people? How will they be helped to develop a sense of belonging to their local community? Appropriate answers will have to be found to these questions in order to implement the policy of teaching urban children in English and selecting the best area language for them.

The existence of inter-ethnic marriages in Uganda further complicates teaching in the mother tongue. As we speak now, there are families where the mother is an Acholi, the father a Mukiga, the baby-sitter a Muganda, while the family is settled in a village in Mbale working with an NGO. Although children are quick to pick up new languages, a child born into such a multilingual home may have a problem of disassociating the different languages and may well develop his/her own new language out of the many he/she is exposed to. The early school days of such children could be very strenuous, and the children might even end up confused. Moreover, policy makers have to bear in mind that the number of children born into multilingual homes is increasing rapidly. Thus, while implementing the policy of teaching children in the mother tongue, such children should be given special attention.

A further problem is that many mother tongues have as yet no writing system, while others that have orthographies still have little written material. For a language to be studied, it must have adequate literature that can be easily and quickly produced in order to enable those who have learnt to read to continue to apply their literacy skills. Oral fluency without written expression does not produce enough material for use in teaching. Few of Uganda's indigenous languages, however, have been developed in both oral and written forms. There is need, then, to develop orthographies for many languages and to develop a tradition of writing in many more. This must be done as soon as possible because the resource base for different languages is fading away: some informants are too old to be of any use, while the speech of those who are a bit younger has been corrupted by exposure to different language situations.

Language specialists for each mother tongue must also be groomed to design instructional materials. The NCDC has already produced an experimental mother tongue syllabus for primary schools but has not designed materials to go with it. Language teachers have been asked instead to find resource people in their district and to use the District Language Board to develop materials *(Mother Tongue Syllabus for Primary Schools,* p. 6); but such language boards are either dormant or non-existent in most districts. Even for those languages that have relatively well developed writing systems, instructional materials are not available at all levels. For example, Luo and Runyakitara are both studied at Makerere University (see Byakutaga and Musinguzi, Chapter 9, on Runyakitara), but little is available for use in secondary or primary schools. Luganda is the only indigenous language for which instructional materials have been designed for all levels, from pre-primary to Master's degree.

Finally, teachers must be trained to use the mother tongue as a medium of instruction in primary schools and to teach the area languages. Yet in the primary teachers colleges (PTCs) such languages are not taught. Teachers trained in English are expected to teach children in the mother tongue. The course content of PTCs thus has to be changed so as to cater for as many indigenous languages as possible. This will pose a very big problem, unless teacher training is decentralised according to mother tongue locations and, as Keshubi (Chapter 8) shows, such decentralisation is hardly practicable.

So where should we begin with teaching in mother tongues? Should we begin with training language specialists at the universities, as Byakutaga and Musinguzi suggest? Should we start at the PTCs with training teachers for the primary schools, as described by Keshubi? Or should we begin at the primary level so as to form a firm base for language learning in PTCs?

Many dilemmas, then, must be confronted if we are to implement the policy of teaching in the mother tongue. We need to address these dilemmas immediately because teaching in the mother tongue will enhance permanent functional literacy in Uganda and, in turn, contribute greatly to our economic development.

EIGHT

The Teaching of Local Languages in Primary Teachers Colleges in Uganda

Hope Keshubi

Mention of the teaching of mother tongues almost inevitably sparks off heated arguments on "which tongue?" and "whose tongue?" Such controversy does not come as a surprise because language is one of the key means by which we are identified; it gives us a sense of belonging or of being left out. In Uganda the case is particularly complicated because there is no single local language that is spoken by all Ugandan ethnic groups, nor is there at the moment any national language. The local languages are, of course, fully adequate to their users: each is a perfect means of expressing the culture of the people who speak it. In this paper, I will discuss the controversy surrounding the teaching of the local languages under the Primary Education Reform Programme (PERP) in primary teachers colleges, and I will present some of the major problems associated with it.

The language situation in Uganda

Bagunywa asserts that "any attempt to use a foreign language as a medium of instruction, at least in the early grades of the primary school, is bound to have a detrimental effect on the child's mental development" (1980, p. 50). He further points out that children's desire to express themselves spontaneously is greatly interfered with if they are using a foreign language:

> Even if he [sic] is to speak a little English, the African child simply cannot be expected to verbalise a foreign language. In any case, such a language may have no "idiom" for expressing his experiences. He cannot find words for the stories he wants to tell … Hence, he says either little or nothing when called upon to speak. (p. 50).

Other educational research shows that it is easier to master the difficult skills of reading and writing in a language that is fully familiar—that is, usually, the mother tongue. Once children are literate, they can learn a second language more easily because they can use their reading skill as a tool for learning it.

With these considerations in mind, it is the policy of the present government of Uganda that a child's mother tongue should be the medium of instruction in the lower primary grades. But if this policy is to be effected, it goes without saying that the country needs teachers who are trained to handle the teaching of the mother tongues. I will now describe Uganda's primary education reform; and the attempts that have been made to implement the government's policy on teacher education.

Uganda's primary education reform

Uganda's education system has been in desperate need of reform since the early seventies; hence the concern of the government in setting up the Education Policy Review Commission in 1987. This commission called for a re-examination of the teacher education courses in the PTCs, NTCs, Makerere University and other universities. The aim was to determine how the existing teacher education courses could produce teachers who would teach more effectively in primary schools, comprehensive secondary schools, and vocational secondary schools. It suggested that refresher courses be held for practising teachers while teacher education courses were adjusted.

The commission's report (Kajubi, 1987) was discussed in parliament and a government White Paper on education was passed (Uganda Government, 1992). Following this, a Curriculum Review Task Force was set up in 1992 under the chairmanship of Basil Kiwanuka specifically to look into the implementation of the White Paper. As a consequence, the government, through the Ministry of Education and Sports, has embarked upon massive reform initiatives, focusing on the primary education system.

The goal of the reform is to improve the quality of education offered to children in schools, but primary teacher education (PTE) has formed a cornerstone of the PERP. The reason is that, according to the White Paper on education, 60 percent of the teachers in primary schools are untrained. The training of untrained teachers, as well as the upgrading of trained ones, must be a high priority, since in the final analysis, it is the teachers in the classroom who are the curriculum implementors, evaluators, and potential innovators, and it is they who, through their interaction with learners, give practical meaning to the curriculum.

The PTE programme is designed to enable all trainees to perform effectively as both classroom teachers and educational mobilisers in the communities. The course focuses on ensuring that each teacher trainee has grasped the minimum learning outcomes in the areas of academic knowledge, production skills, cultural values, language competence, professional education, school practice, and community service. It is run by TDMS, funded by the World Bank, in collaboration with the SUPER project, funded by USAID under the Academy for Educational Development (AED). One of the innovations undertaken by the TDMS programme is on-the-job training of licensed teachers throughout the country. Within this innovation, the re-introduction of the teaching of area languages and mother tongues in the PTCs is seen as a vital requirement.

At the secondary and tertiary levels, students must take up another local language—an area language—other than their own. Hence, five area languages were officially recognised for use in the education system. These are Luganda, Runyakitara (Byakutaga and Musinguzi, Chapter 9), Luo, Lugbara/Madi, and Ateso/Akaramojong. In the PTCs an attempt is being made to introduce the trainees to the area languages in a bid to help them teach the mother tongues in the primary schools. Let us focus on the problems that TDMS/SUPER have faced in trying to implement this policy.

Problems faced in the teaching of local languages

To begin with, TDMS and SUPER have been charged with producing self-study modules to serve as an alternative education delivery system and to provide better quality training and equity of education for the primary school teachers. These modules will be used nationwide to enhance professionalism and to foster interest and a sense of purpose among primary school teachers throughout the country. But teaching the local languages presents its own problems, as Sanyu (Chapter 7) has shown. For purposes of this discussion, I will highlight the following:

Existing written literature
One of the major problems that TDMS/SUPER have faced is lack of enough written literature in the mother tongues on which to base the materials for teacher trainees. Worse still, there are some languages that do not even have standard orthographies. In order to take off, we had to make do with the languages that are somehow established, which means focusing on the area languages. This solution is less than ideal, for, whereas the school curriculum is supposed to cater for the teaching of the mother tongues, the PTCs are not in a position to prepare teachers to do so.

Trained teachers

Even after limiting ourselves to the area languages, we were faced with the problem of identifying trained teacher trainers to handle the writing of both the curriculum and the materials. Most of the writers we identified could read and write their mother tongues but were not well equipped with the skills of teaching. This created difficulties especially when it came to classifying and chunking information so as to make it accessible to learners. The problem indicates that we need to embark on a massive teacher training programme to help this country develop a sufficiently trained force to teach the mother tongues and area languages in the PTCs.

Assumptions

The policy that we are trying to implement is based on certain assumptions that we find, when it comes down to practical action, are oversimplifications. For example, there is a general belief that there is a language known as Luo and it is designated as one of the area languages. But according to the specialists TDMS/SUPER invited to write its curriculum and study materials, Luo is not a language but a language family. Within this family we have, in Uganda, Acholi, Alur, Dhopadhola, Kumam, Lango, Chope, Jonam, Kebu and Lendu (Uganda Government, 1995). For purposes of producing the PTE training materials, the writing team focused on only four of these languages, namely Acholi, Alur, Dhopadhola, and Lango so the speakers of Chope, Jonam, Kebu and Lendu are not catered for. Similar problems have been encountered with Runyakitara (Byakutaga and Musinguzi, Chapter 9).

Another assumption is that since particular languages are spoken in particular districts, each college would cover the language of the district in which it is located. But the TDMS/SUPER colleges cover a number of districts. I will take the example of Loro Teachers College which covers Apac district and Kibanda county in Masindi district. It was assumed that since Loro is based in Apac district, where Lango is spoken, the college would use the Luo modules; but it was later discovered that this would disadvantage the students in Kibanda county, who would be better served by the Runyakitara modules. The case was even more complex in Nakaseke Teachers College where, in what was presumed to be a predominantly Luganda-speaking community, there were many trainees whose mother tongue is Ateso. The main question that arose here was whether training should address the mother tongues of the trainees themselves or those of the students that they were to teach.

Conclusion

It is evident that there is a serious need to review the implementation of the national policy on local languages. There are also more particular needs: training for teachers, including refresher courses after they have been teaching for a while; writing and publication of literature in the mother tongues; public discussion of the problems on radio and television; and the restoration of local language committees. Only with determined action in these areas will the policy of teaching in the mother tongues be successful.

NINE

Developing Runyakitara as an Area Language

Shirley Byakutaga and Rwakisarale Musinguzi

Runyakitara is a name given to the four main Bantu dialects of the western and southern parts of Uganda, namely Runyoro, Rutooro, Runyankore, and Rukiga. They are characterised by a high degree of mutual intelligibility, considerable phonetic similarity, and a significant proportion of shared items in their lexicons. Ladefoged, Glick, and Criper, for instance, put the percentage of shared vocabulary at:

Runyoro-Runyankore	:	86 percent
Rutooro-Runyankore	:	86 percent
Rutooro-Rukiga	:	85 percent
Runyoro-Rukiga	:	87 percent
Runyoro-Rutooro	:	93 percent
Runyankore-Rukiga	:	94 percent

They also observe that Runyoro-Rutooro and Runyankore-Rukiga can each be regarded as "a single unit totalling over 21 per cent of the country as a whole" (1971, p. 71). This view echoes that of Maddox who, seventy years earlier, maintained:

> The difference between the language as spoken in Toro and in Unyoro ... is of no account; and although dialectic differences occur in Lunyankole [sic], in Lunyamwenge [sic] ..., it will be found that any accurate translations into the language of Tooro will be immediately intelligible to natives of Toro, Mboga, and Unyoro up to the Murchison Falls ... (1902, p. 1)

Development of Runyoro as a written language

The missionaries who came to Uganda in the late nineteenth century were instrumental in encouraging literacy in Ugandan languages. Most CMS (Protestant) missions required converts to be able to read in their own language as a precondition of baptism, and although the White Fathers (Catholic) did not have the same requirement, they nevertheless conducted some literacy classes. With regard to western Uganda, these missionaries (and colonial administrators too) believed that Runyoro was the main language spoken in the region and that it comprised several dialects, including Rutooro, Runyankore, Rukiga, Runyakyaka, Rugagya, and Rugangaizi. They consequently devoted resources, time, and effort to developing a written form of Runyoro into which they translated the Bible and prayer books for the use of people in the whole of western Uganda.

The dominance of Runyoro was further manifested in the 1948 Education Report which stated:

> The language policy of the Department with regard to the use of the major vernaculars has remained the same, namely that six African languages are accepted as educational media in the primary school. These are Luganda, *Lunyoro* [*sic*], Lwoo [*sic*], Ateso, Lugbara, Swahili [*sic*]. (Quoted in Ladefoged et al. 1971, p. 91, our emphasis)

From Runyoro to Runyakitara

In the 1940s, Uganda's colonial administrators felt the time was ripe for the introduction of standardised orthographies of some Ugandan languages (the International African Institute of the London School of Oriental and African Studies had already elaborated on the standard orthography of many languages of the Bantu family). Accordingly, in 1946, R. A. Snoxall organised a conference for the western region to deliberate on the orthography of Runyoro. The conference was held at Virika, Fort Portal, and was attended by representatives from Bunyoro, Tooro, Ankole, and Kigezi. It was at this conference, according to Ndoleriire,

> that the representatives of Ankole and Kigezi stated categorically that their language was different from Runyoro and that accepting this new orthography would bring about the demise of their own language which was already developing written materials (1990, p. 40).

Consequently, in 1947, the Education Department authorised the use of Runyankore as a medium of instruction in P1 and P2 in Ankole and Kigezi. The 1963 Castle Report also recognised Runyankore-Rukiga as one of the six major vernaculars to be used in the school system, with Kiswahili having ceased to be recognised as such in 1952 (Kasozi, Chapter 4).

On 24 July 1952, in a conference held at Hoima and attended by representatives from Bunyoro and Tooro and chaired by R. A. Snoxall, the name of Runyoro-Rutooro came into being, while in the sixties the name "Rutara" was recommended for the whole group of dialects since they are spoken "in the area of the former Kitara kingdom" (Ladefoged, Glick, & Criper, 1971, p. 69).

In October 1990, the then Department of Languages at Makerere University, one of whose primary objectives is to develop and teach the major indigenous Ugandan languages, introduced Runyoro-Rutooro-Runyankore-Rukiga as a degree subject. The subject was called Runyakitara, and it is this composite that was recognised as an area language in the Uganda government's White Paper on education of 1992.

Runyakitara as a cluster of dialects

As already noted, Runyakitara comprises a number of dialects spoken in western Uganda and beyond, and, moreover, each of these dialects is itself a dialect cluster. If Runyakitara is to be fully incorporated into the lower levels of the education system, then, there is a problem as to which dialect to teach to whom. For instance, should teachers who speak Runyankore-Rukiga be trained in Runyoro-Rutooro as well so that they can teach in Runyoro-Rutooro-speaking areas and vice versa? Even within the same main dialect, for example, Rukiga, there are so many dialects in use. So, of all those dialects, which should be chosen as a medium of instruction in schools? The chosen one would in principle be used in all print matter and mass media. How acceptable would this be to speakers of the other dialects?

The complexity of the situation makes it difficult, too, to develop an orthography. Standardisation of the written forms of Runyoro-Rutooro and Runyankore-Rukiga has not yet been fully attained. To complicate the situation still further, new orthographies have surfaced over time, and many more may continue to do so, raising questions of acceptability and applicability. For instance, the Runyankore-Rukiga standardised orthography was based on the Ruhima dialect of Runyankole. One wonders whether this orthography will be applicable in Kigezi, as well as in other parts of Ankole.

Instructional materials in Runyakitara

The availability of instructional materials is a crucial issue in implementing the policy of teaching Ugandan children in the mother tongue (Keshubi, Chapter 8). In the case of Runyakitara, there is an amount of available literature, both in Runyoro-Rutooro and Runyankore-Rukiga, for use in primary schools. However, the supply cannot adequately cater for demand if the subject is to be fully entrenched in the education system. Some works need to be reprinted, others to be revised, and new materials must be produced to be relevant to modern needs. Writers must be encouraged to write more in Runyakitara, and also to translate works from other languages. Translation, from Ugandan languages as well as from English, would be a particularly appropriate way of extending the range of Runyakitara literature since it entails cross-cultural exchange and fosters a spirit of cosmopolitanism (cf. Kwikiriza, Chapter 16; Kafeero, Chapter 17).

At Makerere University's Institute of Languages, the unit responsible for Runyakitara has done commendable work in retrieving out-of-print literature and compiling instructional materials. The task of translation is also high on its agenda.

Runyakitara as a university subject

Since its introduction as a subject in Makerere University's Department of Languages (now the Institute of Languages), Runyakitara has had a number of students specialising in it, at both undergraduate and postgraduate levels. The university's School of Education also incorporated the subject into its curriculum in the 1997/8 academic year, and plans are under way to introduce it at the Institute of Teacher Education, Kyambogo, (ITEK), and eventually in all the national teachers colleges in western Uganda.

The founding teachers of the subject were Mrs S.C. Byakutaga (coordinator and teacher of Rutooro), Dr O. Ndoleriire (Rutooro), Dr E. Natukunda (Runyankole), and Dr M.J.K. Muranga (Rukiga). Mr S.A. Mwanahewa and Rev. S. Tumwesigire (Runyankore and Rukiga respectively) also taught it for a while but have since left. Several graduates of the subject have since joined the teaching staff, namely Mr R.M. Musinguzi (Runyoro), Mr C. Oriikiriza (Rukiga), and Mr G. Gumoshabe (Runyankore).

The objectives of the subject at Makerere University are, first, to carry out research in the culture and literature of the Runyakitara language and its neighbouring languages; second, to work with the NCDC and the Ministry of

Education to develop primary and secondary school syllabi for the subject, and with ITEK and NTCs to introduce it in those institutions; third, to organise conferences, seminars, and workshops to coordinate university activities with those of other sectors of society; and, fourth, to liaise with other organisations interested in the development of Uganda's cultures, such as *Tuzimbe Oluganda,* the Luganda Academy, and CHAKU (see Kagaba, Chapter 5). Finally, we aim to sensitise the public, particularly the youth, to the beauty and wealth of their mother tongues through radio, television, newspapers, drama, music, and literature.

Attitudes to Runyakitara

Despite government policies and Makerere's own efforts, the general attitude towards indigenous languages remains an unhealthy one. This is chiefly due to the excessive emphasis on English. For instance, on Tuesday 17 February 1998, the *New Vision* ran a story entitled "Alien tongue makes blacks inferior", in which the author contends that "In order to enhance communication skills and powers, the teaching of the English language should be emphasised from kindergarten to university." He urges Uganda and other sub-Saharan African countries to "… discard, at once, the half-baked and artificial 'nationalist' sentiments" and to "… concentrate on perfecting the usage of the English language." He accuses Uganda's leaders of creating " all sorts of outlandish solutions such as the hyphenated languages (e.g. Runyankore-Rukiga) … some have even gone to the desperate extent of starting new languages from scratch (e.g. Runyakitara)." The author's attitude is representative of the attitudes that shackle the minds of many Ugandans, including parents, teachers, students, and the general public.

However, commendable work is being done by some cultural institutions to encourage people to look more favourably on their own languages and cultures. The Tooro kingdom, for example, through its mouthpiece, the Voice of Tooro, and the Bunyoro Kitara Development Foundation, among others, have set the pace in inculcating in many people pride and a sense of belonging in their own language and culture.

Conclusion

Promoting Uganda's indigenous languages is not, then, without its difficulties, and in view of this, the implementation of the policy in teaching Ugandan children in the mother tongue calls for a multi-pronged attack. Makerere University should be commended for its vigorous campaign in developing and teaching a number of indigenous languages, including Runyakitara. Government, through the Ministry of Education and Sports and other agencies, should seriously encourage other higher institutions of learning and schools at the lower levels of education to take up the teaching of these languages – where there is a will, there is a way.

Part Four

Literacy and Literature: Policy and Practice

Introduction

Basic as orality is to human communication, and vital as radio and television are in modern life, the written word, by virtue of its relative permanence, still has a dominant influence on the perceived status of languages; it is the instrument preferred by policy makers for the direction of language choices in education and by educators themselves for determining what is to be taught. Part Four, therefore, is devoted to the analysis of official policies with regard to written language, especially with regard to its artistic form as literature, and it compares those policies with actual practice, both in and out of the classroom.

In Chapter 10, Kate Parry examines the references made to literacy in the government White Paper on education (Uganda Government, 1992) in order to elucidate how written language is expected to be used and how its use is expected to contribute to national development. She then considers those expectations in relation to literacy practices as they have been recorded elsewhere in the world, particularly in Africa. She argues that literacy cannot be presumed to lead to beneficial consequences; everything depends on the kind of literacy that is in question and on the social practices in which it is embedded.

Rose Izizinga, in Chapter 11, supports this view by showing how the practice of teaching reading in Uganda is not generally calculated to produce independent readers—or thinkers. She focuses on secondary school classrooms, where the typical teacher, in contrast to the ideal one, handles "comprehension" passages in such a way that students have no opportunity to develop their own skill and thus the aims of the government's education policy are undermined.

Chapters 12, 13, and 14 are all devoted to Literature in English, the subject, of all those at secondary level, where reading should be most deliberately and productively taught; and it is also the subject where the humanitarian ideals of education can be most explicitly addressed. In practice, as these papers demonstrate, the subject falls far short of its aims. In Chapter 12, Elizabeth Bakahuuna maintains that literature is grossly misunderstood by the public at large and by students in particular; they perceive it as an arcane mystery accessible only to the most brilliant and of no practical application. Susan Kiguli's description, in Chapter 13, of the ways in which literature lessons are commonly conducted goes far to explain such misconceptions. In many cases, she tells us, students are denied direct access to the texts they are supposed to study, and even when they have such access, they are given no meaningful opportunity to explore them. Rugambwa-Otim, in Chapter 14, attributes the failures of literature, as a school subject, to factors that go beyond the classroom; the problem, according to him, is lack of vision on the part of curriculum planners. Accordingly, he recommends a complete restructuring of the curriculum, one that will encourage innovative and more productive approaches to teaching.

The papers in this part of the book demonstrate a particularly wide gap between the ideals of education and actual practices both in and out of the classroom. They also bring out the point that there are two essential requirements for promoting productive literacy: suitable material, which readers can see as relevant to their own concerns; and lively teachers, who know how to mediate between the oral culture of the students and the written culture of the texts they study. These requirements, more than the mere reduction of illiteracy rates, should be the focus of national and international educational efforts.

TEN

Literacy Policy and Literacy Practice

Kate Parry

"Literacy policy" is an unusual phrase, but it expresses an important concern of educators and language planners. Literacy—that is, the ability to use language in written as opposed to oral mode—is not only a means but also an end of formal education; and it is largely through written texts that language planners try to influence the structure, status, and acquisition of languages (Cooper, 1989). Yet outside academic circles literacy remains a largely unquestioned concept: its necessity and desirability are assumed, but there is hardly any discussion of what it means. My purpose in this paper is to suggest that literacy is a complex social phenomenon, the uses and consequences of which vary greatly in different cultural contexts. Consequently, if policy makers wish to use written language to further their aims, they need to think about how literacy is used and about which of these uses should be encouraged and how, and which, perhaps, should be discouraged and why.

This is not to say that policy makers in Uganda have ignored literacy. On the contrary, the writers of the 1992 White Paper on education mention it no fewer than 48 times, and its converse, illiteracy, a further nine. They also express quite clear attitudes and intentions on the subject: illiteracy is an evil to be eradicated (Uganda Government, 1992, pp. 8, 18, 176, 177-9), so a primary aim of the education system is to teach everyone, both children and adults, how to read and write (pp. 40, 176); literacy, especially as taught to adults, should be "functional" and not just "basic" (pp. 15, 16, 18, 39, 40, 176, 178); it should also be "permanent" and "developmental" (pp. 16, 18, 38, 40, 176, 178). The languages of literacy are also considered: in both adult and primary education, literacy should be taught not only in the local language but also in Kiswahili; while primary pupils should be taught to read and write in English as well (pp. 21, 41). Finally, the government commits itself to definite action to "eradicate illiteracy" (p. 179): an adult literacy campaign will be initiated (p. 178), UPE will be established, and public libraries and rural presses will be set up (pp. 184-5).

There is little to quarrel with in such a policy, but a close examination of its terms raises a number of questions. First, and most fundamentally, why must illiteracy be eradicated? The point is never explicitly addressed, though illiteracy is listed as a problem "related to backwardness and under-development" together with "mass poverty, poor sanitation and health facilities, … poor housing, lack of good water, bad roads [and] diseases" (p. 21). In associating illiteracy with poverty, the White Paper echoes the received wisdom of the international community; it was established more than thirty years ago that a high rate of illiteracy is correlated with, for example, a low gross national product (Phillips, 1970, pp. 24-25). It has never, however, been established that the teaching of literacy will of itself lead to economic development. In fact, the UNESCO Regional Office for Education in Asia has suggested that: "Although they have learned to read, many literate people continue to behave as illiterates" (quoted in Phillips, 1970, p. 26), while a study here in Uganda demonstrates that literacy as taught at the time had virtually no effect on the rural economy (Omoding-Okwalinga, 1985).

The White Paper implicitly acknowledges this problem in its insistence that literacy should be "functional". "Functional literacy" has been defined as "the ability to use reading and writing skills sufficiently well for the purposes and activities which normally require literacy in adult life or in a person's social position" (Richards, Platt, & Weber, 1985, p. 168). But this is a relative definition: what it means in practical terms depends on how written texts are actually used in a particular society. To promote functional literacy in Uganda, then, we need to establish what "the purposes and activities which normally require literacy" in this country are. I would suggest, too, that functional literacy as so defined is not enough, for the point is not to perpetuate the social situation but to change it. So we need also to establish what the purposes and activities are which require literacy to improve people's life and social position.

This point leads to a further question: what do the writers of the White Paper mean by their use of the word "developmental" in association with literacy? Perhaps it refers to economic development, in which case it is closely associated with the word "functional". It may, however, include the idea of personal development and be thus linked to a broader and loftier ideal that the paper invokes, "the intellectualization of all the people" (pp. 15, 16). Again, it is impossible to quarrel with such a vision; but as with economic development, there is no guarantee that literacy will of itself lead to intellectualisation. Numerous studies have demonstrated that the cognitive effects of literacy may be minimal if the range of texts is limited or if these texts are used in restricted ways (see, e.g. Baker, 1993; Bloch, 1993; Goody, 1968; Scribner and Cole, 1981; Street, 1984, 1995). In some cases, indeed, attempts to impose an alien form of literacy through schooling have had the effect of stifling intellectual development rather than encouraging it (see Collins, 1986; Heath, 1983; Michaels, 1986). Thus, "developmental", like "functional", literacy can only be successfully promoted if those responsible have a clear idea of which uses of written text they have in mind and on which existing practices such uses can be built.

The last of the adjectives that the White Paper uses in collocation with "literacy" is "permanent". The significance of this word is much more obvious: it refers to the well-known fact that people who have been taught to read and write all too often forget these skills after the period of formal teaching is over (Abadzi, 1994). The question, then, is how to encourage newly literate people to keep on using written text. One answer is suggested by the White Paper: provide libraries and rural printing presses. The White Paper does not, however, suggest what material the libraries should stock or the presses print, beyond saying that it should be in regional languages and Kiswahili. Those who implement the policy need to think in much more detail than that. What kinds of written text would be sufficiently attractive for people to take the trouble to go to the library and borrow them? And what kinds would be considered important enough for people to buy when there are so many other things to spend money on?

So far I have raised a number of questions about how written text is used, or, to use the expression preferred by many scholars, about literacy practices (Baynham, 1995). What are the existing literacy practices of ordinary Ugandans and how can these practices be productively developed? I am not able to answer these questions right now, for the necessary research has not yet been done, but I can suggest broadly what the answers might be.

A fundamental point established by studies of literacy in practice is that there are many kinds of literacy; some scholars even talk about literacies in the plural (e.g. Barton, 1994, pp. 38-40). These literacies may be associated with different languages and hence with different speech communities and textual traditions. They may have totally different social functions and equally different ideological implications. Finally, they may involve quite different ways of approaching written text and using it in relation to oral language, and hence they may result in radically different reading behaviour on the part of individuals (Parry, 1993, 1996).

What, then, are the dominant literacies in Uganda? The one that most people will think of is undoubtedly what I call "schooled literacy"—the literacy that people encounter first in primary school and then develop through their years of secondary education. It is a literacy that, despite the policies of initiating instruction in the mother tongue and of teaching Kiswahili, is still closely associated with English, and through that language it gives access to people and texts that are essentially foreign. This literacy has a powerful social function, for through the mechanism of exams, it controls access to the metropolitan social structure and hence modern international culture. In short, it plays a significant role in class formation and, incidentally, in siphoning off successful individuals from the rural areas. Finally, because exams are so important in this kind of literacy, there is some danger that it will encourage only a limited kind of reading, one in which the reader struggles alone with the text and tries to learn and understand every word, but does not then apply the information in any practical way (Hill & Parry, 1992, 1994).

Much more could be said about schooled literacy, but it is already extensively discussed, including in the 1992 White Paper itself and in the remaining papers in this volume. I would like to turn to the other literacies that are also important but less recognised. The first of these is "bureaucratic literacy", the literacy of government offices and other administrative institutions. Like schooled literacy, it is closely associated with English (although at local levels of administration, local languages are used), but while in colonial times it represented a direct link between Ugandan individuals and the British government, now it primarily links Ugandans with the central administration based in Kampala.

For ordinary people the link is expressed through documents such as application forms, receipts, and formal letters. Many of these documents are quite mystifying even for those with well established schooled literacy, and the files in which they are kept are not only important instruments of social control but also a means of personal gain to those through whose hands they pass. Anyone who has registered a vehicle or applied for a driving licence will appreciate that this form of literacy is not always constructive, however essential its role in administration may be. It would be worth while, then, to focus attention on how it could be streamlined and made more accessible to ordinary people; and it would also be valuable to consider how schooled literacy might be adapted to prepare people better for dealing with bureaucratic uses (and misuses) of written text (Milton Rwabushaija, of Kakoba NTC, is at present doing research on this issue).

Two other forms of literacy that I would like to comment on are "commercial" and "technical literacy", the former including the use of invoices, receipts and commercial accounts, the latter the use of technical plans and instructions. These literacies are not so closely associated with English. Commercial documents can be written in any language shared by buyer and seller, and for their own accounts sellers can use whatever language they like. Similarly, craftsmen may use their own language in drawing up plans for their own use, as Scribner and Cole describe a Vai-speaking carpenter doing in Liberia (1981). Instructions, of course, can only be read in the language chosen by the manufacturer of the goods in question, but while such instructions are often in English, for many goods, especially those manufactured in Kenya, they are written in Kiswahili as well. Health instructions, too, are often in local or regional languages, a point that is at present being investigated by Jane Alowo.

Whatever the language, commercial and technical literacies are essentially practical in function: they should serve more than any other to promote economic development. We know little, however, about how written text is actually used in Uganda in the accomplishment of practical tasks. Omoding-Okwalinga's study, indeed, suggests that it is not used much for this purpose at all: the literate craftspeople he interviewed did not use their literacy to extend their skills but learned instead, like their illiterate counterparts, through oral means (1985). There may, however, be more commercial and technical literacy in the environment than we think. Recent studies of literacy in Morocco and in South Africa document a wide variety of uses of written text for practical purposes, even, through the help of mediators, by people who consider themselves illiterate (Wagner, 1993; Prinsloo & Breier, 1996, especially the articles by Mpoyiya & Prinsloo, Breier & Sait, and Kell); such literacy practices need to be investigated here as a basis for determining how best to make schooled literacy more practically relevant.

Next, I would like to point to what may be the most deeply embedded form of literacy in this country: religious literacy. This literacy is complicated because the three major religious groups that are represented in Uganda have traditionally used written text in quite different ways. For Muslims, the sacred text must always be presented in Arabic and ideally it should be recited rather than read; the written text serves mainly, then, as a mnemonic. For Catholics, too, the sacred text and accompanying liturgical material, though in written form, are made accessible through oral means, but there is less emphasis in this tradition on learning the text by heart. The Protestant tradition, on the other hand, lays particular emphasis on individuals reading the text for themselves (Byakutaga & Musinguzi, Chapter 9), which means that it must be rendered in the individual's own language and learning to read becomes an essential religious activity.

Despite the differences, the three kinds of religious literacy have important similarities in function. They all provide the basis for a belief system and guidance for personal conduct, and they all foster community membership at both the local and the global level. They all, also, are deeply embedded in local life and provide opportunities for leadership and public respect to many individuals who are otherwise denied them (cf. Gibson, 1996). Religious literacy may thus have a deeper attraction for many, especially among the less educated, than any other kind of literacy. Its characteristics are well worth studying, and the institutions associated with it should certainly, as the 1992 White Paper on education suggests (p. 176), be more closely involved in general educational efforts.

Finally, I would like to touch on the idea of "creative literacy". It is this kind of literacy that I think is meant in the White Paper when it refers to "the intellectualization of all the people", and it is this kind of literacy that is invoked more broadly—though rarely explicitly—by writers who claim the potential of literacy as a means of effecting social transformation (e.g. Freire, 1972). What I am calling creative literacy includes, of course, creative writing, and I am happy to note that a number of new works of fiction and poetry have recently been published in Uganda (Keshubi, 1997; Kiguli, 1998; Kyomuhendo, 1996; Ocwinyo, 1997); and it also includes, to my mind, expository writing, whether in the form of memoirs (e.g. Museveni, 1997) or scholarly studies (e.g. Kasozi, 1994). It is not only writers that are creative, however; at its best and most productive, reading is a creative activity too, as is amply demonstrated by Hill (Chapter 18).

Here, however, there is real cause for concern, for the signs are that although other kinds of literacy are quite well established in Uganda, creative literacy is confined to a tiny élite. New books are being produced, but as the publishers will attest, their sales are pathetically low. "Literature" is offered as a school subject, but so few students take it that Rugambwa-Otim (Chapter 14) describes it as "endangered", and those who do take it depend, all too often, on notes rather than on the actual texts (see Bakahuuna, Chapter 12; Kiguli, Chapter 13). Students who enter the university can obviously read, but they are inordinately dismayed, even at the postgraduate level, if their lecturers decline to tell them what they must know and ask them to read it instead. And many educated people hardly do any reading at all once they have received their qualifications (Bakka, Chapter 15).

It has been argued, convincingly, that one reason why creative literacy is so hard for people in Uganda (and other parts of Africa) to achieve is because it is too often demanded in an alien language, in this case English. But, despite the efforts described by Byakutaga and Musinguzi (Chapter 9), not enough is being done to encourage creative literacy in indigenous languages either. In the past, writers such as Kagwa (1912, 1952, 1953) and Ngologoza (1967) gave new expression to their people's tradition by writing in Luganda and Rukiga respectively, but that tradition has not been continued and their works are difficult to obtain (although Ngologoza's book was reprinted in 1998 in an English translation). Such new writing as is being done in indigenous languages is geared rather to the needs of schooled literacy (Keshubi, Chapter 8) and, while schooled literacy should lead to creative literacy, it all too often signally fails to do so (Izizinga, Chapter 11).

While this survey of literacies in Uganda is by no means comprehensive, enough has been said to suggest that literacy policy requires more careful consideration than it has yet been given. It needs to be based on a realistic appraisal of existing literacy practices and on a sound understanding of the relationships between oral and written uses of language. It needs to take cognisance of the different kinds of literacy and to explore how each is related to personal and social development. It needs, in addition, to consider what materials already exist and how more could be produced and made available for the promotion of the various literacies in question. Finally, as part of a broader education policy, it needs to address the role of formal schooling in promoting constructive literacy practices. As Izizinga points out, traditional methods have for too long prevailed in the schools' teaching of reading, producing students who are "literate" in the sense that they can read aloud but who are effectively incapable of learning from written text. Literacy policy, then, on the part of not only government but also NGOs and leading educational institutions, must first be fully articulated before it can be effectively implemented in the design of curricula, the production of materials, and, last but not least, the training of teachers.

ELEVEN

The Teaching of Reading in Uganda

Rose Izizinga

When the Educational Policy Review Commission was appointed by the Ministry of Education in 1987, one of its main concerns was how individuals could be equipped with basic skills and knowledge to exploit the environment for personal as well as national development, for better health, nutrition and family life, and the capacity for continued learning. To this end, the commission recommended and the government agreed to:

- establish permanent literacy and numeracy in local languages;
- equip individuals with knowledge, skills and values for productive work;
- provide a channel for post-literacy continuing education;
- develop in individuals the desire and capacity for self-development and an interest in life-long learning;
- provide prerequisites for continuing education and development; and
- enable people to develop adequate practical skills for making a living. (Uganda Government, 1992)

While these may represent different kinds of literacy (Parry, Chapter 10), they all presuppose the teaching of reading. The national policies cannot be successfully implemented, then, without a clear understanding of what reading is.

The concept and significance of reading

As Urquhart and Alderson (1987) point out, reading involves at least two elements: reader and text. The interaction between these two is a normally silent mental activity in which individuals draw on their own perceptions as they negotiate the material before them (Rivers 1981, p. 59). The process leads readers through what Goodman (1967) has described as a psycholinguistic guessing game, while Williams (1984) and Nuttall (1984) both characterise reading as a process of obtaining meaning from written text, for a purpose.

While the purpose of reading may be for pleasure, it can be and is more importantly employed for more serious functions; in particular, it is fundamental to formal education. As Francis Bacon put it, "Reading maketh man perfect", for it enables the getting of information from written forms (Nuttall, 1984). Bright and McGregor argue that reading is the core of the English language syllabus:

1. Books provide most pupils with the situation in which learning takes place. Where there is little reading, there will be little language learning ...
2. Only by reading can the pupil acquire the speed and skills he [*sic*] will need for practical purposes when he leaves school. In our literate society, it is hard to imagine any skilled work that does not require the ability to read ...
3. Further education depends on quantity and quality of reading ...
4. General knowledge depends on reading ... (1971, p. 52)

The two authors go on to assert the importance of literature in the enterprise of teaching reading:

5. ... In most schools there is ... a desire and a need to read texts of literary worth for their own sake ...
8. It is in literature that the student is most likely to find words used memorably with force and point ... (1971, p. 53)

Unfortunately, a growing number of literature students do not have the urge to read. They wait for the teacher to read for them, which retards the students' own progress. Such learners cannot acquire the skills with which to understand and enjoy written texts.

Traditional teaching of reading

An explanation for students' reluctance to read can be found in the way in which reading has traditionally been taught. Most teachers assume that they "possess" their classes and adopt a teacher-centred mode of teaching, assuming the role of experts who have to perform all the time. Most are probably ignorant of the true concept of reading, confusing "reading comprehension" with "reading aloud" and apparently unaware that learner involvement is the key to learning how to read. Their conception of their role as teachers, together with their failure to understand what the reading skill entails, leads them to usurp the learners' role. During reading lessons, they take it upon themselves to read to and for the class, even when the pupils have the same text in their hands.

Alternatively, for the sake of varying their methods, teachers make the pupils read to the class in turns. After reading aloud, such teachers then make the pupils discuss answers to the comprehension questions set on the passage before the pupils attempt any silent activity. What actually goes on in such lessons is very unrewarding. Apart from practising their listening skills, the learners have been given no chance to learn how to read nor even a purpose to listen for. The so-called reading lesson benefits only the few who practise reading aloud. When the class discusses the answers to the questions on the reading, there is no reading comprehension done, even though that is the intended purpose of the lesson. The learners leave the classroom having learned no reading skill at all.

When students in the Bachelor of Education and postgraduate diploma in education programmes at Makerere University were asked why such practices are so widespread, they offered the following explanations. With regard to teachers' common practice of reading aloud to the pupils:

- Teachers read to the class in order to help pupils' reading task.
- It assists quick understanding.
- A lot of work can be covered in a shorter time.
- It gives pupils the chance to listen for pronunciation.
- Unavailability of the reading materials is part of the cause.

As for why "turn taking" is practised, the responses were:

- Students gain confidence when reading aloud.
- Teachers can correct their pronunciation.
- The books are not enough.

On why some teachers make pupils discuss comprehension questions before the written exercise is done, these were the responses:

- To cut down on the number of mistakes the pupils are likely to make.
- To help the weaker ones understand what the text is about.

From these responses, it is clear that teachers who work in this way are unaware of the concept of reading. For them, all reading is reading aloud. They have no clear aim of teaching how to read and do not know the appropriate method of teaching the skill. They may also be lacking in patience and commitment.

When the same informants were asked whether there was a period on the timetable allocated to reading, the answers were:

- There is so much grammar to cover in such a short time; therefore, no time for reading as such.
- Reading is a luxury; there is no time to spend on it.
- We teach only what is examinable; the skill is not examined by the UNEB.
- There are no books for reading.
- Once in a while when there is no teacher to occupy a class, pupils may read on their own.

Again, most of the answers show that many teachers are unaware of the concept and the importance of reading comprehension. Others are convinced that reading as a skill is sufficiently covered by dealing occasionally with comprehension passages in class. It seems they have no notion of extensive reading, nor are they aware of the valuable language learning that is derived from reading widely.

Pupils handled by such teachers can hardly acquire reading skills. They do not know when to skim, scan, read with moderate speed, or slowly for the purposes of study, nor do they have referential, interpretive, or predictive skills. The effect on literature or literary studies is that pupils tend to leave all the work to their literature teacher to read and dig up information from the texts for them. They neither read the texts, nor make notes on their own. It is no wonder that at the end of the literature course candidates do not score very highly. More broadly, and still more seriously, the pupils of traditional teachers can hardly acquire the permanent literacy and numeracy that the White Paper on education advocates. A few of them may by chance develop a love for reading, but in the society as a whole a reading culture cannot develop. And, in failing to develop a reading culture, education is failing to contribute to progress and to fruitful exploitation of the environment.

Ideal teaching of reading

Today, however, many teachers are changing their views about their role and are becoming aware of the value of reading in the learning process. They are beginning to see that, ideally, their task is to help their pupils to accept and assume their responsibility as learners and to become fully involved. They realise that it is this involvement that will later facilitate the pupils' advancement into self-sufficient and useful citizens. They conduct their reading lessons by rejecting the role of performer and instead accepting a variety of other parts:

- *Conductor.* Teachers direct the learning process by providing the reading materials, pointing out the skills to be aimed at, and seeing that the learners are practising these skills appropriately.
- *Organiser/Monitor.* Teachers plan activities so that learners can have the opportunity to practise reading meaningfully, individually, in pairs, or in groups. Teachers also check to see how the learners are carrying out the activities.
- *Stimulator.* Teachers perform this role when they try to get learners to react and interact. Class interaction encourages oral fluency as well as involvement with the texts read.
- *Consultant and manager.* In this role, teachers act as points of reference for their pupils, answering questions and solving problems as they arise.

In assuming these roles, modern teachers will endeavour to stock a range of reading materials and create time to read them.

Pupils of such ideal teachers are able to read intelligently, interpret, analyse, infer meaning, predict situations, and achieve a lot in a small space of time. They acquire study skills and can learn on their own. They love books and find time to read them; they build up their own collections as well as getting acquainted with the library; they read fluently and fast when necessary, but read examination questions carefully and perform well in response to them. These readers not only learn more language (in this case English) but are also able to use their skills to learn any subject with ease and interest. They can find their way about in life and can also lead their neighbours. Such individuals will always march with the civilized, academically, socially, and politically; they are equipped to become Bacon's "perfect man".

TWELVE

Literature: Addressing Misconceptions

Elizabeth Bakahuuna

Literature is embedded in the life of all citizens, whether schooled or unschooled, for it comprises not only the written texts that are selected for academic study, but also the riches of our oral traditions: songs, proverbs, tongue-twisters, stories—the folklore, in short, which everybody shares. The theme of literature is life in all its aspects, and its sub-themes are such universal issues as culture, birth, death, and love. And literature is also language, that is, the use, adaptation, enhancement, and even violation of language for the purposes of assimilating, interpreting, and building on the delights and the horrors of human experience. No wonder, then, that thoughtful intellectuals have struggled to keep literature on the school syllabus, not only as material to be learned but also as a means to learning.

The set texts that are used in teaching literature in Uganda reflect well this grand conception of the subject. On the one hand, they expose students to many different cultures and ways of life. In Chinua Achebe's *Things Fall Apart,* students read about the custom of casting away twins and about the white man's condemnation of the custom; thus they have to weigh the values of one culture against those of another. In Shakespeare's *Merchant of Venice*, they encounter the transaction by which Shylock lends money against the surety of the right to take a pound of flesh—again, a challenge to their values, for such an agreement is repugnant in African society where property is never valued above human beings. On the other hand, students perceive in these texts widely varying uses of language. Okot p'Bitek's language in *Song of Lawino* seems obscene to some, but it effectively conveys in English, a typically Luo flavour, with Luo perceptions and values, and thus students can learn to appreciate rather than criticise it. The language used by Ngugi wa Thi'ongo in *Petals of Blood*, is quite different, while that of Charlotte Bronte's *Jane Eyre* is of course different again, so in reading these works, students begin to see how language reflects and gives form to culture.

71

The public, however, has its own attitude towards literature and its teaching, an attitude that reflects a complete failure to understand what it is about. For example, at an occasion that I attended a few weeks ago, an MP and government minister who was the guest of honour advised parents against letting their sons and daughters go to university to study language and literature. He said that economics is a better subject. He failed to see that knowledge of economics is useless without the language to express it, and, indeed, that to understand social interactions, including economic ones, one needs some understanding of human emotions and beliefs. Similarly, when I interviewed some of my colleagues in the PGDE programme, they tended to make a false distinction between "literature" and "English language". According to one student of maths and physics, "Literature is quite different from English. It is a mere burden." The remark reflects a widespread failure to appreciate that the aims and teaching of literature and language are inextricably intertwined.

These attitudes are common among the schooled public. Those who are unschooled have a different view, but it is still based on a misunderstanding. They tend to hail and praise the educated simply because they "can read", while those who have just a little schooling give exaggerated deference to literature students, considering them to have greater wisdom than others. This kind of deference again fails to take account of the universal nature of literature and of its close relationship to orature and traditional culture.

Why do such misunderstandings exist? It is partly because so many parents pay for their children's education without any understanding of what that education is about. They see the skills obtained from schooling as no more than the ability to write official letters and read newspapers, and as nothing to do with the understanding and appropriate conduct of personal and social relationships.

But literature teachers themselves contribute to the misunderstanding. They do not know the aims and objectives of teaching literature, even though each school has a copy of the syllabus book, because they consider only the question of what they should teach rather than the question of why they should teach it. They are not creative in their teaching; on the contrary, they teach everything according to the set texts, either word for word or else through notes, often using published notes for the purpose. These notes fail to take the students' level of understanding into account and do not constitute any meaningful communication about the real literature themes. Students who are taught in this way naturally study the subject only to pass exams and qualify for further studies, while those who do not offer literature simply dismiss it as difficult to understand and no more than a waste of time.

There are, however, some exceptions to this pattern. Some teachers try to make literature a part of their English language teaching, making it lively and thus contributing to the students' general performance. They draw on the students' own knowledge and experience; for example, in one lesson that I attended, the teacher helped us to understand Dennis Brutus's poem, *Somehow we survive*, by having us discuss our own memories of war. Some teachers, such as Rugambwa-Otim at Makerere University, also draw directly on the resources of orature using drama and music in their English literature lessons. Other resources are available too: the radio, audio- and video-tapes, and visual illustrations in the form of charts and pictures. The teaching of literature does not have to be as unsatisfactory as it is.

So what practical steps can be taken to improve the situation? First, I think it is important to convey to all teachers (of whatever subject) a sense of what literature and English are and of how they can contribute to all academic study and to nation building more generally (see Rugambwa-Otim Chapter 14); similarly, students need to be informed about the aims of the subject beyond the mere passing of exams. Second, all students should be able to learn literature—it should not be reserved for only the brightest; and to make the subject accessible to larger numbers and weaker students, teachers should be prepared to improvise materials where necessary and to be imaginative in their use of teaching aids. Third, as Kwikiriza (Chapter 16) suggests, the teaching of literature should be linked more closely with traditional orature through the use of drama and music. Fourth, and perhaps most important, teachers should not just rely on their own notes and textbooks but be prepared to elicit and respond to the students' ideas.

To conclude, literature should be able to create awareness and appreciation of one's own language and culture as well as introducing one to another language and other ways of thought—and English language and literature in particular, should be able to promote understanding and cooperation all over the world. Thus, literature should be seen as essential not only to the educational, but also the economic and technological development of a country. Such a subject demands more teaching materials and better classroom teachers; above all, it calls for an alert type of teacher who is prepared to do much more than merely follow instructions.

THIRTEEN

Reflections on the Teaching of Literature in Ugandan Schools

Susan N. Kiguli

Literature, the Irish poet Yeats once said, "is the greatest teaching power of the world." Its materials have stood the test of time and evolved with the times, and they offer varied and numerous lessons on the fundamental issues of human existence. "Literature has been called the mirror of mankind, the channel of culture, the fine art of verbal expression" (O'Grady, 1974, p. 20). The importance and relevance of literature to society seems well established; the claim that it is crucial to the curriculum makes sense. It is vital, then, that it should be taught clearly and carefully and in accordance with the aims of including it as a school subject. Yet from informal discussions with secondary school teachers, it seems that there has been no conscious effort to use these aims to guide their approaches to teaching literature. Most teachers can hardly remember the national aims of teaching the subject; they just work in the spirit of "this subject has been given to me and teach it I will." They generally teach in the way they were taught themselves, making no effort to analyse or evaluate the approaches available and the students' responses to them. This paper argues that teachers need to reflect on both the general aims and their own individual approaches if literature is to be taught effectively.

The national policy stipulates that the aims of teaching Literature in English are to provide knowledge about world literature through study of various selected works, to widen and enrich the students' written and spoken English, to encourage the development of a reading culture (something that has so far eluded us), and to sharpen the learners' judgement and analytical ability. These aims, though general and rather broad, will, if taken seriously, greatly influence the approaches adopted in teaching literature and encourage a more involved and analytical attitude towards the methods that teachers use.

So, what are those methods? A survey of a few schools in and around Kampala revealed that most teachers adopt the traditional classroom role in which they transmit information about the authors and the texts to the students. The students play a passive part, being expected simply to understand the mysteries expounded to them. Apart from robbing the students of the opportunity to participate in interpreting the text, the teachers impart their knowledge in an incomprehensible fashion. They tend to emphasise critical commentaries over the primary works so that the students are denied direct contact with the poems, plays, and novels being taught. In this approach, the teacher gives lengthy explanations about the author, the background of the work, and the socio-historical circumstances that inform it. The students are turned into ardent little note takers who do not even stop to understand what is being said. The result is a massive loss of interest in the subject as students conclude that "Literature is undecipherable; one cannot understand it even on close reading."

Sometimes, if the teacher is dealing with a more advanced class, the tendency is to expound critical terms and techniques of writing without even providing background information or illustration. A teacher may, for example, list a number of poetic terms such as metaphor, metonym, parallelism, etc., in no particular order and with a long definition of each. The effect on the students is somewhat frightening. Many who encounter this kind of teaching resort to listing all the terms they know beside a poem or piece of prose even before they read through it; they then look for metaphors, similes, etc., in the piece without stopping to consider what it offers in itself. Sometimes in responding to a text, students force these terms onto it, ticking them off one by one until they are satisfied that they have said something on all the terms and techniques they know. One of the major objectives of reading literature is to derive pleasure; but in this process, pleasure is easily killed.

There are cases where teachers do expose students to primary works of art but the teaching is still not effective. Some go to class with one of the set plays, novels, or poems and make one student after another read aloud without any specific motive or goal. The students chosen to read often do it badly or without any interest, because they are outside the work and share no part in it; the others get so bored that they lose interest in the class altogether. So by the end of the chapter read (and in some cases the lesson may end before the chapter is through) the students have gained no significant or valuable experience.

In some classroom situations, especially at the advanced level, some teachers adopt a more student-based approach. In such cases, the teacher divides the class into various groups, provides questions, and asks the groups to discuss them and present a write-up of their discussion to the class. This approach would be helpful if the teacher had previously given the students some exposure to the body of established knowledge about literature. But, in many cases, the students operate in a kind of vacuum, having nothing but their own resources to draw on. In this approach, too, the students are not helped to develop constructive or critical thought.

If the general aims of teaching literature are to foster pleasure in reading and to enrich language learning as well as increase knowledge of world literature, there is need for intimacy between the teacher and student in the working environment. Teachers need to think of ways in which the work can become part of themselves to enable them to offer it meaningfully to the students. They should be sensitive to the class's needs and moods and should make it easy for the students to interact with them. As Galavaris has noted:

> Teaching is giving yourself. Beyond the facts of knowledge, beyond books or papers or exams there is something else which is the most important of all. It can only be described as a love affair between the teacher and the students. It is this relationship which creates the necessary climate in which the student grows, and the teacher finds meaning for what he [*sic*] is trying to do. (1974, p. 6).

Teachers should show love for the subject, a deep interest in what they teach, and should share this open enjoyment of the subject with their students. Or, as O'Grady has said: "What I do as a teacher originates partly in the belief that if one treats a good poem, or short story, or drama with due respect, with reverence, it will reveal its aesthetic goodness" (1974, p. 19). It is assumed that once the students realise the beauty of the subject, they will derive pleasure from it and with pleasure will come love for literature and for reading.

To sum up, I would like to suggest that to promote interest in literature among their students, teachers ought to emphasise primary works over critical commentaries. The students should be encouraged to come in direct and intimate contact with the poems, plays, and novels being taught. They should be geared towards discovering these works for themselves, to get fascinated and involved in the texts' meaning. So, even in large classes where discussion may be difficult, it should still be tried in varied forms; students can, for example, be given questions beforehand so that they find out the answers from reading before being asked to address them in class. Teachers, for their part, need to realise the importance of both the reader and the text and of the interaction between them. They need to know both their subject and their students and constantly to study and review their material and their teaching methods in the light of the general aims of teaching and of the changing situations in their classrooms.

FOURTEEN

An Endangered Subject: Literature in English in National Integration and Development

Rugambwa-Otim

The advent of Europeans, "discovering" this part of Africa and colonising us, saw the introduction of a formal education system with a curriculum that served their own interests. The British, as our colonial masters, introduced English Literature with the aim of inculcating their own cultural values so that we could emulate them in everything they did. They had a focus and they succeeded. In embracing English, Ugandans accepted cultural values embedded in that language. The aping of many English ways is still with us: our females still, for instance, value slimness as beautiful and bleach their skins. The English literature curriculum was, however, a hidden one—that is, it was undefined for Ugandans. The colonial education authorities never had a written teaching syllabus but simply issued a list of books for both "O" and "A" levels, together with an examination syllabus. The question now is whether this hidden curriculum has effectively changed. When Ugandans attained political independence, did we receive educational independence as well? If we did, did we nurture it? Did it flower and bear fruit?

When self-government was established in African countries, English Literature was replaced by Literature in English. It encompasses literature from across the world, whether written directly in English or translated from other languages. The idea was and still is to introduce learners to a wide range of cultures. Yes, but what is the focus? We continue to teach a list of texts, without a teaching syllabus, apparently for no better reason than that those of us brought up in the English tradition of scholarship would like to see it continuing. As a result, as Jude and Jude say, "Literature in English ... is seen as isolated and élitist, something only the better [learners] can pursue with any degree of success. Most importantly—and disastrously—Literature in English is perceived as something otherworldly, having little to do with 'real life'" (1995, pp. 110-11).

The problem is that the purpose of teaching literature is not clear even to curriculum planners, teachers, and examiners and, still less, to students and the communities from which they come (cf. Bakahuuna, Chapter 12). Let us then redefine the role of Literature in English in the light of seven national goals for education:

1. *Forging national unity and harmony.* This implies three kinds of national integration; we need to integrate Uganda's various ethnic groups to form one nation; we need to integrate its social classes, reducing the gap between the élites and the masses; and we need to integrate our values, evolving a national value system out of a multiplicity of ethnic ones.
2. *Upholding and maintaining national independence.* To achieve this, we need to foster patriotic feelings—a sense of love for all Ugandans and a readiness to make sacrifices in defence of the country's unity and sovereignty.
3. *Promoting moral and ethical values so that we can live in this competitive world harmoniously.* These values include honesty, responsibility, integrity, accountability in the use of public funds and property, love for productive and constructive work, and respect for those who labour to produce wealth.
4. *Promoting humanitarianism and cooperation.* These qualities depend on self-esteem as well as concern for others, and a philosophy of selflessness rather than self-seeking as a basis for working with fellow Ugandans and with other people the world over.
5. *Evolving democratic institutions so that every citizen has a voice in governance.* This vision includes sensitising and empowering students by ensuring their effective participation in organising their own activities and in developing social services for the communities where their schools are located.
6. *Guaranteeing fundamental human rights.* Students need to be taught their rights and how to defend them within the framework of the national constitution and the White Paper on education.
7. *Creating national wealth.* The achievement of this goal rests on the development of the students' cognitive, affective, and psychomotor faculties so that they can acquire productive skills and build integrated and self-sustaining personalities. People so educated will be creative, and as such can contribute to the development of an independent national economy.

Literature in English ought, then, to empower students with skills needed to help the nation achieve these goals. First among these are language skills: listening, speaking, reading, and writing should be at the forefront of literature classes. As Povey says, "Literature will increase all language skills because [it] will extend linguistic knowledge by giving evidence of extensive and subtle vocabulary usage, and complex and exact syntax" (1972, p.187). In particular, though, Literature in English must be explored for the development of reading. Moore quotes Cox's point that learners "can be helped to develop emotionally, aesthetically and intellectually by means of the pleasurable activity of reading. The pleasure principle should motivate the programmes of study and always be given a high priority" (1990, p.135). Reading and Literature in English enhance each other because, given direct access to appropriate texts (Kiguli, Chapter 13; McGregor, Chapter 2), learners will be motivated enough to enjoy reading.

Studying literature, however, is more than developing language skills. It also calls for and develops cognitive skills at various levels: knowledge, comprehension, application, analysis, synthesis, and evaluation. It develops affective skills too, requiring the perception and expression of emotions, cultivation of interest as well as empathy, and judgement of values (cf. Bakahuuna, Chapter 12). Psychomotor skills are also involved, because studying literature entails reciting, acting, dancing, and singing. And literature teaches social skills, enabling one to fit in any community through an enhanced understanding of human relationships. Beyond all this, Literature in English is an excellent vehicle for imparting and developing fundamental values: awareness of human rights combined with a sense of social responsibility; appreciation of social equity and of democratic participation in decision-making; understanding and tolerance of cultural differences and pluralism; compassion, cooperation, and a spirit of caring; enterprise, creativity, and open-mindedness to change.

However, to achieve these purposes, Literature in English needs to be taught within the framework of a curriculum that spells out guiding principles commensurate with the nation's needs. After all, literature is the artistic use of words to capture an image of humanity and human relationships. Learners should not merely perceive but fully absorb this relationship between literature and society so that their reading of literature texts can help them in solving personal, societal, and national problems. Thus, Literature in English must be made relevant to national, regional, continental and, finally, global situations; no text should be taught unless it has application for the learner and society.

For this reason, I am suggesting a complete shift from the present curriculum to a *thematic approach:* let us start by choosing themes that we consider important for self and group identity; then texts can be chosen and grouped around these themes. Possible themes include:

* respect for human dignity, knowing the self, adaptability;
* loyalty, patriotism, nationalism, respect for values, cherishing one's origin;
* decisiveness, assertiveness, leadership; and
* cooperation, unity.

The first of these themes is geared towards developing self-esteem and self-knowledge; the second towards promoting a sense of belonging; the third encourages participation in decision-making; the fourth focuses on collective responsibility. As for the texts, any that addresses an assigned theme can be used. For example, the theme of cooperation and unity can be explored through reading any of the following: Golding's *Lord of the Flies,* Camus' *The Plague,* Orwell's *Nineteen Eight-Four,* Keshubi's *Going Solo,* or Tindyebwa's *Recipe for Disaster.* The approach would require a student to read as many texts as possible to demonstrate an understanding of the theme and the ability to relate the texts to everyday life.

For the curriculum outlined to meet the needs of learners and of society, the whole teaching process has to change too. If Literature in English is to play its rightful role in national integration and development, the stereotyped approaches have to be done away with and new approaches adopted. Teaching based on giving students notes (Kiguli, Chapter 13) must stop, and students must be guided to study and interpret the texts by themselves. As UNESCO has recommended, teachers should be helped "to adapt to more modern approaches such as democratic participation in the classroom, cooperative learning and creative problem-solving [and to] use the latest array of innovative and interactive pedagogic methodologies" (1996, p. 194). Through these new pedagogies, and with a more appropriate curriculum, we can breathe life into this endangered subject. We can make Literature in English friendly to the student, and we can make studying it a joyous adventure rather than an intellectual chore for the sake of passing exams.

Part Five

Creating a Reading Culture

Introduction

The 1999 conference, on "Reading and writing creatively", was not unnaturally more forward-looking than the previous one: rather than criticising present practices, it focused on ways in which such practices might be changed so as to produce more creative uses of written text. As it happened, most papers considered reading rather than writing (though a number of the workshops were devoted to writing skills). Accordingly, the group presented here can be considered collectively as describing how, from the present situation in Uganda, we can develop a reading culture.

In Chapter 15, Father Peter Bakka presents a clarion call: "Back to books!" As a professional librarian, he offers advice as to how we ourselves can read more, and more productively, as well as on how we can encourage others to do so. He emphasises the importance of libraries, as collections of books, in this endeavour, but insists that social activity around written text is equally important—thus reinforcing the point made by Professor Parry in Chapter 10 that our focus should be not so much on literacy itself as on the development of productive literacy practices.

Father Bakka relates literacy to orality through such practices as reading aloud. Following this theme, Loyce Kwikiriza and Ibrahim Kafeero emphasise the relationship between literature and orature. Ms Kwikiriza suggests that creative writing, and hence reading, can best be encouraged by asking children to draw on the rich oral resources of their own cultures and languages, and she gives a specific example, from Runyankore-Rukiga, of the kind of material that might be used. Similarly, Ibrahim Kafeero argues that the best approach to the problems encountered in Literature in English (see Chapters 12, 13 and 14) is through traditional orature. Specifically, he shows how the figures of speech used by modern African poets echo those of oral poetry, including such familiar forms as lullabies and children's games. Approached through such forms, literature should no longer be seen as alien and difficult.

Clifford Hill's presentation completes this collection with a fuller exposition of such ideas. He first demonstrates how young children are naturally creative in their reading, but that the practice of assessing reading ability through exams all too often requires them to suppress that creativity. He then shows an alternative and potentially more productive mode of assessment. At the same time, he argues for the use of traditional oral materials in reading instruction and assessment, not only because such materials are familiar but also because, while being simple in form, they are rich in content.

In emphasising the use of traditional oral forms, these chapters suggest an approach not only to the problems of literacy discussed in Part Four, but also to those of multilingualism discussed in Parts Two and Three. For example, Hope Keshubi (Chapter 8) has lamented the difficulty of finding writers in the mother tongues. If, as Ms Kwikiriza suggests, teachers would encourage their students to write down and translate material collected from the elders of their own people, this problem would be partially addressed. Similarly, Rhoda Nsibambi (Chapter 3) has pointed to the social tensions that can arise from people of many different cultures and languages having to live together. If, as Professor Hill suggests, teachers and students from diverse backgrounds can pool the traditional resources of their own peoples, they will bring out and emphasise the common humanity of all. We hope, then, that the papers in this part of the book will encourage its readers to draw on all the country's linguistic resources— oral as well as written, in local languages as well as in English – to develop a reading and writing culture that has firm roots in local traditions while its branches reach out to a wider world.

FIFTEEN

Back to Books: Functional Literacy

Peter Bakka

If our schools are not nurturing a culture of reading and writing creatively, what are they here for? As a professional librarian and religious adviser of Masaka Diocese, I visit schools regularly, and, in the presence of their teachers, I ask the students four questions. The first two run like this: "How many of you know how to read?" They all laugh at me. Of course they all know how to read! Then I go on to ask: "How many of you have ever picked up a book and read it, not for examination purposes but for some other reason?" In the more than thirty secondary schools I have visited, I have come across none where more than ten students answer that question in the affirmative. When I ask the same questions with regard to writing, the situation is worse; some senior secondary students in day schools have never written even a single letter on their own. So the failure to read and write creatively begins right from our schools. All of us who are sick and tired with the state of literacy in this country need to link up arms and together cry, to ourselves and others, "Back to books!"

Dr Thangaraj has rightly said, "He who does not read is no better than he who cannot". Or, to put it another way, those who know how to read and write but do not do so in their daily lives can be described as "functional illiterates" and I think you will agree with me that of all Ugandans who are literate, only a small percentage can clearly escape this label. However busy, a functionally literate person reads at least one book a month. I guess all of us here know how to read and write in principle, but would I not embarrass many if I were to ask the question here and now, "How many books have you read this month?" Traditionally, literacy has been tied solely to winning jobs and attaining promotions, so we have fallen into the trap of "mechanistic literacy", whereby after school, little or no reading is done, or such as is done is of newspapers not books. As for writing, hardly any takes place after school at all. A good many of us Ugandans are so learned, yet so illiterate.

The fight against illiteracy cannot succeed, then, without a collateral fight against functional illiteracy. We have to struggle together to make reading and writing part of our general culture and individual behaviour. So we must work at once to implement the following recommendations:

Building libraries

The word *library* stands for two things, the *building* and the *library material.* The tendency to stress the building as more important ought to be avoided. A library is not a shrine for the worship of books, but should be, to modify the famous metaphor of Socrates, "the delivery or maternity room of ideas", a workshop for creative reading and writing. And it is possible to build most of the libraries we need in a short time if we abandon the philosophy of "Can't". The frequent use of "I can't" is more often than not a substitute for "I can't be bothered to try." There are lots of unused books lying around in our society. No one is asking for them. Also, millions of books are shredded, burnt, or allowed to gather dust in publishers' warehouses all over the world. Most of these could be given out free if one politely asked for them, and they could form the basis for various types of library.

Let us begin with *school libraries.* Our schools deserve better libraries than they generally have at present. The type of learning we have in our schools is what one may rightly call "textbook learning", and the type of teaching "textbook teaching". That is why, up till now, a student can reach Makerere University or any one of our other universities without ever needing a proper library, where he or she can explore a subject beyond the information that is given in class. When schools begin to acquire real libraries, the system of education and teaching will have to change radically. It is interesting to note that in the United States of America, research calling for creativity in reading and writing begins right from nursery schools. Here in Uganda, if research begins at all, it is at the post-secondary level. Needless to say, students who begin research early are set to become creative readers and writers and thus real productive nation builders.

But we need more than school libraries if we are to escape the problem of functional illiteracy. The secret of the success of the European, American, and Japanese democracies is the *public library* where every citizen finds the vital information needed in making well-informed and therefore mature decisions in daily life. "An ignorant society is indeed a vulnerable society" (Herman Ssemuju, personal information, 1994). One of the most urgent demands we should make of our politicians is to have a public library in each county, built and maintained on the tax-payers' money. The "public libraries" available at the moment are in fact school libraries in disguise. We need to work for public libraries worth the name.

Public libraries can be supplemented by *personal* ones. People with personal books should begin to lend them privately to the less privileged. As Andrew Carnegie says of Colonel James Anderson:

> Colonel James—I bless his name as I write—announced that he would open his library of 400 volumes to boys, so that any young man could take out, each Saturday afternoon, a book which could be exchanged for another on the succeeding Saturday. And the future was made bright by the thought that when Saturday came a new volume could be obtained. (1948, pp. 43-44)

"But," people here will tell you, "all the books will be stolen." A person who knows the history of libraries knows that this is nothing new. The answer to this problem is called the *one way library*. With such a library, "If someone brings back the book, he gets another, if he never brings it back, he gets no other." We must be willing to have many such libraries if the struggle to make reading basic to our culture is to bear fruit. Here we have to make George Sand's words our own, "Know how to give without hesitation, how to lose without regret, how to acquire without meanness".

Finally, let me mention the idea of a *home library* . This may be no more than a cupboard or a number of shelves with books for both young and old in the family. If for no other reason, books are essential in a home with a new born baby. Children need to be allowed to play with books, for the sooner they become accustomed to the sight of the covers, bindings, and pages, the sooner they will begin to develop the concept that books are part of daily life.

Reading aloud for children and adults

"The first and most important instructor in composition," says Clifton Fadiman, "is the parent, older child, or teacher who reads aloud to the small child." A child is not deaf, dumb, stupid, or vegetable-like. It hears a story on at least three different levels, intellectual, emotional, and social. The first sound it hears is a poem: the rhythmic beat of its mother's heart.

The Russian poet and literary historian Kornei Chukovsky describes every child's capacity for language between the ages of two and five as "near-genius" (1963, pp. 7, 9), and by age thirteen children have usually reached their language development peak. Therefore, for at least twenty minutes every day, children should be read to. If this is done, only illiterate parents would have to take their children to school to learn the first A, B, C. As you read to the little baby, you help fight beforehand the "reading is work" mentality. Be short but constant. The best time is before lunch and before bed. Let the finger do the walking and talking by lightly running it under the words you read. Dramatize the story line, producing sound effects (ready to knock on a table or wall where the story calls for a "knock at the door").

Read-aloud programmes should be organised to target every child in the areas we come from. Volunteers should be obtained to read to children who might otherwise not have a reader within the family. At public libraries, capable people should read books to children and to illiterate adults, as well as to literate ones who have no time to read for themselves. Schools should, among other things, invite parents and community members during a regular Book Week to read a story to the class. This should inspire children to know that reading is not just for kids at school but for everyone.

Introducing SSR

Sustained silent reading (SSR) is the natural partner of reading aloud. SSR was originally proposed in the early 1960s by Lyman C. Hunt, Jr, of the University of Vermont in the USA. It consists of reading silently for ten to fifteen minutes every day, at home or in class, for example before lessons begin in the morning. It has particularly great impact if done by the entire school, involving teachers, students, secretaries, cooks—everyone. In SSR each person chooses what to read for the period; the only constraint is that the reading should be done and that it should be silent. I tried it with my "A" level General Paper class every Friday morning, when I also came with a book, like the students, and read. The fruits in creative reading were innumerable.

Raising public awareness

"It is the responsibility of people who carry torches to pass them on," Plato, the Greek philosopher, once said. Let each one of us vigorously or even aggressively get engaged in public awareness, selling book-reading as we sell political candidates. First, proclaim the value of books in themselves: they are portable, noiseless, can be enjoyed anywhere, any time, and by any age group and, as Carlyle said, "A true university these days is a collection of books." Then, point to the personal gains from reading them. "You open doors when you open books," says William A. Peterson, and so he exhorts us, "Read to lead, read to grow." Or, again, Aldous Huxley declared, "Every man who knows how to read has it in himself to magnify himself, to multiply the ways in which he exists, to make his life full, significant, interesting," and Henry David Thoreau was making much the same point when he commented, "How many a man has dated a new era in his life from the reading of a book?" (See Tucker, 1989).

These and similar quotations can be used as slogans to be put on T-shirts and posters to support a general literacy campaign. At the same time, we should organise small seminars and workshops on reading in the schools, local councils, professional offices, dioceses, banks, etc. Big names in entertainment such as Fred Ssebatta, Matia Luyima, and Kafeero should be explicitly and specifically requested to compose songs, singing the praises of reading books and writing creatively. The role of libraries in creative reading and writing should not be overlooked: one of the things that needs to be done in this public awareness campaign is to introduce to secondary school students (and teachers) the subject of library and information science as a serious profession; and the question of giving reasonable salaries to librarians and including it in the schools' and other institutions' budgets should be looked into as a matter of urgency.

Making time to read

All our preaching will be ineffective, however, if we, who claim to be well educated, do not read ourselves. If you are one of those who find no time to read because you always have a busy schedule, allow me to pass on to you some suggestions made by Lydia Roberts in the *Boston Globe*. First, she says, talk less. How much time do you spend in trivial conversation? Couldn't some of that time be spent reading? Second, always carry a book with you. Then whenever you have to wait, whether it be for a taxi, or in the bank, or at some official's office, you can put the time to good use—and the waiting, incidentally, becomes less tiresome. Third, put a book under your pillow at night, and when you can't sleep, read. Similarly, keep a book handy to pick up in the kitchen, your dressing room, or by the telephone. Our lives are full of odd moments which can be used profitably if we always have a good book to hand and read it whenever we have nothing else to do.

Finally, let us conclude with H. H. Barstow's great library users' prayer:

> Lord, make me respect my mind so much that I dare not read what has neither meaning nor moral. Help me choose with equal care my friends and my books, because they are both for life. Show me that as in a river, so in reading, the depths hold more of strength and beauty than shallows. Keep me from caring more for much reading than for careful reading, for books than the Book. Give me an ideal that will let me read only the best, and when that is done, stop me. Repay me with power to teach others, and then help me to say from a disciplined mind a grateful Amen.

SIXTEEN

How can Reading and Writing be Built on Oral Traditions and Practices?

Loyce Kwikiriza

People derive a sense of identity and belonging first, from the language that brings them together and second, from their culture – that is, what they do, whether it be art, music, or any other activity. If language and culture are not passed on, then the people concerned have no tradition and thus no basis for their own behaviour. In Africa, at least before the coming of the missionaries, the culture was passed from generation to generation through oral tradition and practice; that is, the people's wisdom and the language itself were transmitted by word of mouth, while traditional practices were learned by the young generation observing closely what their elders were doing.

There were several forms of oral tradition. There were stories, for example, which were mainly told in the evening around the fire. They were not told just for the sake of it; each had a purpose, to teach morals and give warnings to children about the dangers of misbehaviour. Then there were proverbs or wise sayings which were intended to instil wisdom in the young generation and help them grow into sharp wise elders. For example, the older people among the Banyankore-Bakiga used to refer to unwise naive youths as *okuriire eryo* or *okuzire buroro*. The terms emphasise the fact that the young people, though fully grown, were still childish and immature. To keep their youths in check, the Banyankore-Bakiga used proverbs such as *Oyefundikiire kubi, embeba nizija kukurya*, which means literally, "If you don't cover yourself properly, rats will eat you"; in other words, you should check your behaviour lest you earn an unbecoming character in society. This proverb was addressed especially to girls, who were expected to grow without any speck so that they could marry well and in turn bring up morally upright children.

In addition, there were riddles, tongue twisters, metaphors, similes, and idiomatic expressions, all of which made the language rich and uniquely identified with a certain class of people. In Ankole and Kigezi, it is rare for someone to utter three sentences without using a simile or some metaphorical description such as, *Ndi ekyoma*, "I am iron"; *Ni entale*, "He is a lion"; or *N'amate*, "She is milk" (that is, good or beautiful). A good Runyankore or Rukiga speech is supposed to be flavoured with proverbs; it is a style normally associated with elders, but even the youths have taken to it. The Banyankore-Bakiga also have vows such as, *Ninkakurye, Ninkainare,* and *Ninkaterwe enkuba* which can be translated respectively as "I would rather eat you", "I would be damned" and "I would rather be struck by lightning." These vows were used to reinforce promises, and surely once they were uttered, the promises would be honoured.

The cultural practices were daily and occasional events in which young people had to either participate directly or watch closely what was being done. Each cultural practice carried significance. There were songs and dances for particular occasions: *ekimandwa* for appeasing spirits, *ekizino* for marriage ceremonies, and *ekitaguriro* for beer parties. Then there were several rites and ceremonies that were performed, such as the mourning ceremony when somebody died, or the slaughter of a ram to avert bad luck when twins were born. The funeral rites for unmarried people were particularly interesting. There was a practice known as *okugyera empango* where an unmarried male would be made to sleep with a banana stem before his burial and a lady with her brother before her burial to prevent the spirit of that person from haunting the family members—for they believed that the spirit of a person who had never entered marriage could not be appeased.

All these traditions gave the Banyankore-Bakiga a sense of belonging and helped them to identify themselves confidently with their place of origin and their language. These things united them and built them up from generation to generation because they were passed on either by word of mouth or by practice. So how can we use them to develop a culture of reading and writing? It is high time we started paying due attention to the knowledge of the elderly folks, because they still hold these precious traditions of long ago. Unfortunately, they are becoming a "rare species", so we had better use their knowledge now. This knowledge should be written down, pieced together, and preserved for future generations.

Of course it is understood that different peoples in Uganda have different cultural practices; but this is all the more reason to devote time to the collection of all oral traditions, regardless of background. The traditions can be married together, to make every reader identify the piece of writing with his or her own culture, which will make reading all the more interesting. It can be easily done through inter-school or inter-regional traditional material presentations.

It can be presented orally and then written down, of course not forgetting to reward the best presenters as a way of motivating them to do better.

We also need to look at the language that should be used. If possible, writing and reading, based on oral tradition and practice, should remain in the original language because only that language can fully express the cultural and social inheritance of the people that use it. For the purposes of those who do not understand the language and for whom a foreign medium has to be used, the original expressions should still be incorporated; they can be quoted as they are, with explanations, or else they can be literally translated in the style of such writers as Chinua Achebe or Okot p'Bitek. It helps the readers to understand the culture of the original language and even to compare it with their own. These readers can be the next writers giving us their own traditions and practices.

Writing competitions, based on oral traditions and practices, should be encouraged in schools such that young writers are trained and a writing and reading skill is built early enough. So story telling in the lower primary classes should be supplemented by reading and writing traditional poems, songs, and stories in upper classes. When these skills are fully developed at an earlier stage, then oral tradition and practice can be a rich resource. Students should also be encouraged to translate stories, poems, and songs either from their mother tongues to English or vice versa. These translations should be in written form so that readers of either language can benefit.

Similarly, to make a successful piece of writing, we can create drama in class out of oral traditions and practices. It should have a powerful impact on the students, appealing to both mind and heart. Then teachers or the students, can write a piece from that drama, using the kinds of traditional African expressions that will make it appealing to readers. The students, especially those who have participated in the drama, will thus be trained to use their dramatic sense to write interesting and enjoyable pieces.

When such activities are organised in the classroom, group and pair work should be encouraged since one student may not know enough to work alone; students will need to brainstorm together about what they are going to write, especially if they belong to the same culture. Together they can decide on a story, choose appropriate words to fit different characters, get appropriate metaphors, similes, and speech mannerisms to develop them, and include proverbs and riddles that fit the situation created; in this way they will produce wonderful pieces of writing. They can develop the skills of writing and reading together and, in future, they will be capable of writing independently.

Why is it important to build reading and writing based on oral tradition and practice? First, it will help students to appreciate their own cultures, while exposing them to cultures other than their own. Second, it will teach them to value their own languages as valid means of communication. Third, it will develop their sense of creativity and imagination as they reproduce and modify their material and then develop new material from it. Finally, by helping students communicate from the known to the unknown, it will develop their literacy skills as well as their oral skills not only for English and literature, but also for other subjects.

SEVENTEEN

Mother Tongue Poetry
and the Appreciation of Poetry in English

Ibrahim Kafeero

In Uganda today, poetry particularly refers to poetry in English, which is taught as part of the literature course. The subject is feared by many Ugandan students, even more than other aspects of literature (cf. Bakahuuna, Chapter 12). As David Cook puts it, "Generations have emerged from African schools afraid of poetry because their teachers have been afraid of it, so that it is seen all too often as a tedious and fearsome obstacle which no one would enter upon again of their own will" (1980, p. 35).

The appreciation of poetry does indeed require patience and perseverance. In order to comprehend a poem in the first place, the reader has to attend to the words one by one in correct order, building up basic meanings. Moody describes the process in this way:

> Compare yourself to a pilot of an aeroplane crossing the ocean: suddenly in the midst of the empty space he [*sic*] is aware of an unfamiliar object. He wonders what it is, he goes closer ... eagerly looking for any signs which tell him exactly what he is looking at: every little detail ... may help to bring him an idea. (1987, p. 7)

Having built up an understanding of the poem, the reader can go on to the next stage of appreciation, which involves recognising and isolating the various literary devices used—the choice, order, and sound of words; the use of rhythm and rhyme; the introduction of imagery, allusion, and symbolism—in order to explain their effect. This work of analysis in turn provides a basis for critical judgement; that is, the reader can now make a decision as to whether the poem communicates effectively or not. The process is not a simple one, but it is worth the effort. As Cox and Dyson observe,

The practical criticism of a poem is not the opposite to enjoyment, as students new to it are apt to fear. It is not the substitution of an intellectual pleasure for aesthetic pleasure or the diminishing of poetic understanding to a dull routine. On the contrary, it is the opening up of a poem for what it can really be for us: a unique and fascinating experience ... to those with the patience as well as sensibility to recreate. (1982, p. 13)

Unfortunately, as Kiguli (Chapter 13) has shown, few teachers in Uganda encourage their students to make the necessary effort to achieve this kind of pleasure. Teachers and students alike seem to see poetry as something alien and incomprehensible. They fail to see that poetry has deep roots in African culture. As Cook argues,

With a rich store of oral traditions in the African atmosphere, we have no excuse for looking at poetic form as the rarefied possession of an intellectual élite. Almost all societies find occasions when prose expression is inadequate to achieve the required intensity, when more meaning is demanded in concentrated form ... It is natural the poetic forms should be popular not only at times of public ceremony and ritual, but on most occasions when the community is involved in verbal expression. (1980, p. 45)

What has happened in Africa, according to Cook, is that the printing press has tended "to compete with communal song till the latter has retreated from its public functions, leaving poetry to limited groups of creators and audiences" (p. 47). For children, formal schools have frequently uprooted them from their origins and backgrounds, killing their orature. Yet African societies, especially in rural areas, still depend on orality for communication more than the written word, and modern African poets draw on African oral modes in combination with western literary practices. So following Kwikiriza (Chapter 16), I would like to argue that we need to draw upon our traditional oral resources in order to develop a basis for appreciating modern poetry.

According to Nandwa and Bukenya, oral literature, or orature, consists of "those utterances whether spoken, recited or sung whose composition and performance exhibit to an appreciable degree the artistic characteristics of accurate observation, vivid imagination and ingenious expression" (1983, p. 1). It includes narratives, proverbs, recitations, and songs, all of which are communicated by word of mouth but with qualities we can regard as literary. Different communities have different categories of orature but I will cite those of the Baganda as an example. They are *engero* and *enfumo*, both of which are stories, *engero ensonge,* meaning proverbs, *ebikokko*, or riddles, *ebyafaayo*, which is history, *ebiwanuuzibwa*, meaning legends and myths, *ebintontome*, or recitations, and *ennyimba*, or songs.

According to Finnegan, much of African orature was linked to the "traditional kingdoms of Africa, with their royal courts and clearly marked differences in wealth, power and leisure" (1976, p. 83). Poets and singers were attached to the courts of powerful kings and to those who had pretensions to honour and thus poetic celebration in society; examples are the Zulu and Sotho kingdoms, Bornu, Hausaland, Congo and Buganda. Religious patronage was also sometimes responsible for the development of orature as in Buganda, Bornu, and Hausaland, and also among the Swahili. While traditional African religions, like that of Buganda, promoted songs, Islam promoted poetry, the composers of which had prestigious positions on account of their Quranic learning. Later on, Christian missionaries drew on African oral performances, especially songs, to express and propagate their own teaching.

There were other, less professional, manifestations of orature too, especially in the songs, dirges, and lullabies that were usually produced by women. Lullabies provide good examples of the very beginning of mother tongue poetry. In all societies, they represent a simple, natural, and spontaneous expression of feeling when a mother sings to her child; yet they express society's conventions too. In most societies, it is the mother who has the responsibility of looking after the young one, as the following example from Buganda illustrates:

> *Obukodo bwa nnyoko obwo bunnakuleranga.*
> *Bwafuna akamerere ke "munkwatire"*
> *Bwamala okulya nti "Mumpe eno".*
> *Baa akaliga kanywa taba.*

This lullaby can be translated as follows:

> Ha! that mother who takes her food alone
> Ha! that mother before she eats "Lull the child"
> Ha! that mother when she has finished to eat
> Says, "Give the child to me."
> Baa, the little lamb—the smoker!

There are also rhymes, songs, and recitations for children, or for grown-ups to recite to children, which are distinct from lullabies and ordinary adult songs. Africa has a rich store of verse that is used for play: nonsense and funny songs, singing games, counting games, hide and seek games, and so on. In Buganda, games that are accompanied by songs or recitations include *ekigwo* (wrestling), *omweeso* (bow), *okwebagala* (animal riding), *sekitulege* (children's fiddle), *okulwanyisa amafumu* ("fighting" with spears), *okulwanyisa emiggo* ("fighting" with clubs), *nkusibidde awo* ("detained"), and *nkulimbye* (fool's day). Others, for which I have no translation, are *enje, okukuba malippo, entooketooke,* and *okusiita.* These form a basis for poetic practices to begin and stick in the mind of an individual and in the culture more broadly. Modern professional entertainers, for example, draw on these resources, as Rasta Rob does in *Kaneemu ka nnabbiri* and Afrigo Band does in *Amazzi gennyama.*

Modern African poets also draw on the resources of traditional orature and so they bridge the gap between the printed word and the word of mouth. Foremost among these poets is Okot p'Bitek who developed his series of "songs": *Song of Lawino, Song of Ocol, Song of Malaya,* and *Song of Prisoner.* In these songs, he celebrates Africa's values and freely employs rhyme, repetition, and imagery. Consider the following example from *Song of Lawino:*

> My mother
> Was a well known potter,
> She moulded large pots,
> Vegetable pots,
> And beautiful long-necked jars.
> She made water pots
> And smoking pipes
> And vegetable dishes.
> And large earthen vessels for bath. (p'Bitek, 1972, p. 133)

Or, again:

> The tattoos on her chest
> Are like palm fruits,
> The tattoos on her back
> Are like stars on a black night;
> Her eyes sparkle like the fireflies,
> Her breasts are ripe
> Like the full moon. (ibid. p. 52)

Another poet who draws richly on images and ideas developed in the mother tongue is Ralph Bitamazire:

I love you, my gentle one;
My love is the fresh milk in the *rubindi*
Which you drank on the wedding day;
My love is the butter you were smeared with
To seal fidelity into our hearts.
You are the cattle-bird's egg,
For those who saw you are wealthy;
You are the papyrus reed of the lake
Which they pull out with both hands.
And I sing for you with tears
Because you possess my heart:
I love you, my gentle one. (Cook & Rubadiri, 1971 p. 23)

Here the idiom and culture of Rutooro comes through clearly, although the expression is in English.

Africa, then, has rich poetic resources in its oral traditions, and poets such as Okot p'Bitek and Bitamazire have shown how they can be developed and used in the creation and appreciation of written poetry in English. Teachers and students should be encouraged to take the initiative in building on the poetry of their own cultures. Kwikiriza and Hill (Chapters 16 and 18) suggest ways in which this can be done: for example, a Progress Profile like the one described by Hill could include poetry collected and written down in the mother tongue. It could also, as Kwikiriza suggests, include translations written by the student in English, as well as, of course, the student's own poems in either language. All these poems could be presented orally as well as in writing. Such activity would produce many benefits, as Cook has argued:

> The practical value of poetry is both social and educational. Enjoyment and pleasure form a big part of it, more especially in Africa. Besides, poetry contributes to a learner's psychological life and linguistic skills, serving an educational purpose. (1980, p. 4)

For the benefit of our communities, then, as well as for the individuals in our classes, we should use mother tongue poetry to develop orality as a basis for literacy.

EIGHTEEN

To read is to write: From oral to written culture

Clifford A. Hill

"...reading has killed my man."
Song of Lawino
"...what is the use of a book, thought Alice, without pictures or conversation?"
Alice's Adventures in Wonderland

To return to Africa is always a privilege, for it was here that my career as a teacher began. I am particularly pleased to visit Uganda since, although I have not been here before, it holds a set of compelling associations for me. Indeed, it was an encounter with one of your countrymen that gave me a most memorable lesson on the riches and power of oral culture; and so, indirectly, led me to the theme expressed in my subtitle today. More than 25 years ago, I was invited to a small gathering of African writers and American scholars interested in literary uses of oral material. The weekend gathering was held in a rural inn, and when Sunday evening arrived, we discovered that the road had become impassable because of a heavy snowfall. Some of us— especially those whose culture honours a strict schedule—became anxious about Monday morning obligations, but, fortunately, there was one in our midst who took the delay as an opportunity for celebration. Okot p'Bitek soon had us all laughing—and even forgetting that there is such a thing as Monday morning—as he took us on a journey into various imaginative worlds. As he spoke, he became, through gesture and movement, the creatures that inhabit these worlds—hare, spider, lion, elephant, and all the rest whom you know far more intimately than I do.

As we watched Okot perform, we became aware that not only he but also ourselves were becoming the creatures of his imagination. I was dismayed to discover that, with a slight nod of his head, he had selected me to be the

97

spider who eats up all the food (he had perhaps noticed me returning for a second helping at our evening meal). Such probing, yet gentle revelations of character, helped to bring together a dozen strangers from two distant continents and brought forth our common humanity. When I learned that I would be coming to Uganda, the memory of that evening came back. I felt sad that I would not be able to visit Okot and experience the magic of his storytelling once more, but I am happy that Acholi oral culture lives on in his literary work.

I am pleased that I was invited to speak at a conference that has such an evocative theme: "reading and writing creatively". Most of us associate the word creative with writing rather than with reading. Creative reading strikes us as an odd expression, and I propose that we use this oddity as an occasion to discuss certain aspects of reading that are often neglected, indeed suppressed, by dominant literacy practices in education (see Parry, Chapter 10).

These practices are particularly in evidence in the tests used to determine whether students can comprehend what they read. Let us examine two passages, one drawn from a literary work, the other from traditional oral culture, and both used as part of a reading test. I have deliberately chosen these passages to illustrate, once again, the theme of "from oral to written culture". We will begin with the literary passage, which was prepared for use with children in the third and fourth years of primary school in the United States of America (MacGinitie, 1978; Hill & Larsen, 1999):

> The fawn looked at Alice with its large, gentle eyes. It didn't seem at all frightened. "Here then! Here then!" Alice said, as she held out her hand and tried to stroke it. It moved back a little and then stood looking at her again.

As some of you perhaps recognise, this passage is taken from Lewis Carroll's *Through the Looking Glass*. This work is of particular interest for our purposes, since it took shape, as did *Alice's Adventures in Wonderland*, while its author, a mathematician at Oxford University, was telling stories to entertain the children of a friend. The test makers adapted it slightly, partly, I presume, to set up the tasks, which are of the multiple choice type. Please take a moment to respond to these tasks before we embark upon a discussion of what they require the reader to do.

A)   How did the fawn's eyes look?

sad   gentle
tired   frightened

B)   What did Alice try to do to the fawn?

help it   hug it
pet it   hide it

As you have perhaps noticed, both tasks require readers to carry out local operations. Task (A) calls for a single adjective, *gentle*, to be recycled from the first sentence, "The fawn looked at Alice with its large, gentle eyes." Task (B) calls for the verb *stroke* in the third sentence to be defined as *pet*. Indeed, the point of this task can become clear if it is rewritten as, "In the story, the word stroke means _____ ." Neither task is intrinsically difficult, but each can be confusing, by virtue of one of the four choices provided, to children who are engaged in—and here we can use our odd phrase—creative reading.

In responding to task (A), many children are attracted to the choice *frightened*, since what they know about the world conspires with what is in the passage to give them the sense that the fawn was frightened. Let us first consider what is in the passage. The second sentence states that "it [the fawn] didn't seem at all frightened," which alerts creative readers to the possibility that it was, in fact, frightened. When such readers come to the final sentence, they can find further material that supports this possibility: "It [the fawn] moved back a little ...". Once these two bits of text are brought together with the knowledge that the fawn is an animal likely to be frightened when it encounters a human being, readers are in a position to be attracted to the choice *frightened*.

In interviewing children after they read this passage, we discovered that many of them used textual evidence to support their choice of *frightened*. Consider, for example, the response of an 11-year-old African-American boy when he was asked: "Why did you pick *frightened* as the answer to the first question?"

Because it says in the story when she tried to stroke it, it moved back and looked at her. His eyes were wide open so it must be frightened.

In his response, the boy initially focuses on the crucial textual information—
"it moved back"—that justifies the inference that the fawn was frightened.
But since task (A) is concerned with how the fawn's eyes looked, he goes on
to state that its eyes were "wide open"; this child apparently viewed the fawn
as on full alert because of its fear.

Many children who chose *frightened* for task (A) then chose *help it* for
task (B). In making such a choice, they, once again, brought together what is
already in their head with what is on the page. In reading the passage, they
interpreted not only Alice's words—"Here then! Here then!"—but also her
gesture— "reaching out her hand to try and stroke it"—as evidence that she
is trying to help the fawn by calming its fears. This interpretation is
strengthened by the presence of *try to* in task (B), which can be viewed as a
cue that the question is concerned not simply with what Alice did but rather
with what she was attempting to accomplish with her action. When these two
different kinds of textual cues are brought together with the knowledge that a
little girl is likely to try and help a small animal, readers, especially those
who have selected *frightened* for task (A), are in a position to select *help it*.

Here is how a 10-year-old African-American boy responded when he was
asked why he thought Alice was trying to help the fawn (I stands for the
interviewer and C for the child):

> C: Because it says right here—here it is [he then reads from the passage,
>   replacing *stroke* with *help*].
> I: How do you know she tried to help it?
> C: She tried to stick her hand out for her to reach it.

While reading what Alice said to the fawn ("Here then! Here then!"), he
provided an extremely soothing intonation.

We usually begin an interview by asking children to retell us what they
have read. Here is a retelling by a ten-year-old girl whose family had recently
immigrated from Jamaica.

> Once upon a time Alice was walking through the forest and she saw a fawn. It
> was beautiful and she saw how gentle it was looking at her. So she went over
> there and walked to it and tried to pet it. Then the fawn jerked back. She was
> wondering why did the fawn jerk back. So she went over there and she went to
> get her friend. Her friends came. They all surrounded the fawn and then suddenly
> she got to it. And then she realised that the fawn had a broken leg.

As can be seen, this young girl included in her retelling all the basic information contained in the passage; clearly she was able to understand what she read. Her retelling contains, however, important clues that she recast that information so that it reflects a more complete story. To begin with, she opens with the formulaic "once upon a time". Moreover, she was not content to end, as did the passage, by reporting the fawn as moving away from Alice as she approaches it. Rather she developed the encounter by reporting that Alice and some friends (perhaps she supplied the latter since presumably a young girl would not be alone in the forest) discover that the fawn had a broken leg. At first glance, such an extension of the passage appears somewhat arbitrary, since it contains no information that can be used to infer that the fawn was hurt. But when one considers that the fawn, as a wild animal, was likely to run away from Alice, the way in which she developed the story becomes more plausible: the fact that the fawn was hurt helps to explain why it did not run away.

Let us now turn to a passage based on a story drawn from traditional oral culture. This story comes from New Zealand and was used in that country's Progressive Achievement Tests of Reading.

Here is a little story about a dog and what happened when he was helped by a pukeko

One day when a dog was having dinner, a sharp bone stuck in his throat. Not long after his meal, he began to feel a great pain. He spent a long time trying to get the bone out, but he could not. At last he went to a pukeko and said, "If you take this bone out of my throat I will give you a reward for your work." So the silly pukeko put his long neck into the dog's mouth and pulled out the bone. Then he asked for his reward.

The dog said, "You already have your reward. You should thank me for not biting off your head while it was down my throat."

As can be seen, this passage is, in certain ways, better suited to testing children's reading comprehension. To begin with, it presents a complete story and so children are less tempted to extend it in ways that may interfere with their test performance. It is also accompanied by a picture showing a long-necked bird (the pukeko) with its head down the dog's throat and a brief introduction that helps children develop a context for their reading. Despite these improvements, the tasks still present problems similar to those we have been considering. Below is one of the tasks that accompanies this passage, and again I encourage you to take a moment and respond to this task before you continue reading.

5. This story is **mostly** about a
(A) dog finding a bone.
(B) dog with a sore stomach.
(C) pukeko's reward.
(D) foolish pukeko.

Perhaps you have noticed that this task, much like the ones we considered earlier, sets up a tension between the target response and one of the other choices. The target response is "a pukeko's reward", which requires readers to maintain a descriptive posture toward what they read. Within the stem of the task, the word *mostly* has been placed in bold, which presumably functions as a clue that readers should select the choice that most comprehensively accounts for the passage information. It is, however, difficult to maintain such a descriptive posture, when one of the choices, "a foolish pukeko", stimulates a more interpretive approach. The whole point of the story is that the pukeko was, indeed, foolish to put its head in the dog's mouth (within the story, the pukeko is even described as silly). Consider, for example, how an eleven-year-old Latino girl defended her choice of "a foolish pukeko".

I: Why did you choose (D)?
C: Because he put his neck inside the dog's mouth and that's nasty and that's foolish.
I: Why is it foolish?
C: Because a normal person—or whatever it is—wouldn't actually put his mouth or his head or anything else into the dog's mouth.
I: Okay.
C: 'Cause it could be a trap.
I: What kind of trap?
C: He puts his head into the dog's mouth and the dog just bites it off.

As can be seen, this girl has clearly understood the story and focuses sharply on its main point.

I do not have time to provide further evidence of the ways in which traditional testing requires children to suppress creative reading in order to perform successfully (see Hill & Parry, 1988, 1989, 1992, 1994, for further evidence). I would like rather to turn to the question of whether more appropriate forms of assessment can be developed that allow for greater creativity. In responding to this question, I would like us to consider an assessment programme known as *The Progress Profile*. In order to provide an alternative to traditional testing, this programme was developed as I worked with teams of teachers in metropolitan New York. I will not describe the programme in detail (see Hill, 1992, 1995, for such description), but I would like to show how stories from oral culture are used in assessing children's reading comprehension. In order to contrast our programme with traditional testing, I will present a version of the story we considered earlier. This version is adapted from a Hausa folktale in West Africa (in the original version, the animal was a *dila,* jackal, which, because of his cleverness, Hausa people refer to as the *malamin daji,* teacher in the wild).

> One day a fox was eating a chicken when a sharp bone got stuck in his throat. As he began to call for help, he said, "I'll give a reward to anyone who can get this bone out of my throat." A stork came walking along and said, "I'll help you get that bone out." So the stork stuck his head in the fox's mouth and pulled it out.
>
> The fox then turned around and started to walk away. The stork was surprised and so he asked, "Where's my reward?" The fox answered, "Here's your reward: you stuck your head in a fox's mouth and you're still alive."

After children read this story, they respond to five different kinds of tasks:

Retelling the story
Can you tell me in your own words what you just read?
Factual tasks
Why did the fox need the stork's help?
What did the stork do to help the fox?
Inferential tasks
Why was the stork able to help the fox?
Do you think the stork got a real reward? Please explain your thinking.
Holistic tasks
Write an ending to this story in which the stork manages to get something that (s)he thinks is a real reward. You can either change what the fox did or add something new that shows the stork getting the kind of reward (s)he wants.
Experiential tasks
Describe an experience in which you were disappointed by a reward that you received. Try to explain why you and the other person differed in your thinking about a reward.

As can be seen, these tasks are designed to elicit a broad range of responses. The initial task of children retelling the story provides a baseline from which we can evaluate their responses to various kinds of comprehension questions. Although the task is not designed to emphasise creativity, children still vary a good deal in how they respond. With respect to the first task, for example, certain children tend to summarise the story, whereas others tend to perform it. Consider, for example, how the following two retellings illustrate these contrasting tendencies:

Summary
The fox was eating and...um...he was eating something and a bone got stuck in his throat and after he finished eating it...he felt pain and then he went to the stork—I think it was—and the stork helped him with the bone and took it out.
(10-year-old African-American girl)

Performance
The fox was eating a chicken and he started choking and yelling, "Help! Help! I'll give you a reward." And a stork came and helped him. The fox didn't give him a reward and...um...the stork yelled, "Where's my reward?" The fox said, "You're just lucky to be alive. I didn't bite your head off."
(11-year-old African-American boy)

We do not attempt to mark these different kinds of retelling, though the teachers are provided a form that they can use to record the degree to which (1) the retelling was a summary or a performance, and (2) it included the basic elements of the story. Here is how this form was used to record the summary style used by the girl in her retelling.

Story style Performance Summary	Yes/No	Comments
Story Elements	**Yes/No**	**Comments**
fox gets bone stuck in throat	x	Chicken not mentioned; fox felt pain
fox offers a reward for help		
stork gets bone out	x	
fox doesn't give reward		
stork asks for reward		
fox explains what reward is		

For the factual and inferential tasks, a marking scheme is provided, though even here teachers are encouraged to record any distinctive elements in children's responses. It is important to note that these two kinds of tasks are presented separately so that children will not be forced, as they are by multiple-choice tasks, to figure out whether they should respond at a factual level or an inferential level.

As for the last two kinds of tasks—holistic and experiential—a marking scheme is not provided, since they are designed to elicit more creative responses. Since the responses to these tasks are written, they can be placed in the children's portfolios. Here is an example of a holistic response in which a child extends the story:

> "That is not fair. I did you a favor and I don't get anything." The stork left. A couple of days later the fox got a bone stuck in his throat. He went back to the stork and asked for help. The stork said, "No." The fox begged and begged so the stork said, "If you give me my reward before I do anything, then I will do it." The fox gave him a reward and he got the bone out of his throat.

This child is so focused on making sure that the stork gets the reward before performing the favour that he neglects to mention just what the reward is. As for the experiential task, children vary a good deal in how they respond to it, but a common theme is parents giving them something they didn't want (e.g., a book on science) for performing successfully in school.

As can be seen, the *Progress Profile* is designed to elicit a broad range of responses from children to what they read. It also includes activities in which children create their own stories, but since my focus is on creative reading, I will not describe these activities in any detail. I would like, however, to describe one way in which creative writing is used. After a child has composed and illustrated a story, the child's work is made into a small book through simple bookbinding techniques. A pocket with a library card is placed inside the back cover, and the book is then placed in the classroom library so that children can check out each others' books and take them home to read. After children read a book at home, they write comments in a small notebook that they give to the child who wrote the book. In this way, children are encouraged to engage in social interaction around the stories they write.

Having illustrated how stories from traditional oral culture can be used in alternative assessment, I would like to end this presentation by describing a project, under development at Columbia University, in which a colleague and I are assembling stories from different parts of the world in a curriculum to be used in teaching English as a second language (Hill & Langer de Ramirez, 1999). Although our primary audience is children, we have found that these stories also work well with older learners. We have entitled this curriculum *Why-Stories from Around the World,* since it is built around stories that provide explanation for basic phenomena such as death or the alternation of day and night. Stories are also included that provide explanation for unusual aspects of nature such as the cracked shell of a tortoise. Given the range of themes, the stories encourage laughter as well as serious thought. In particular, they encourage children to observe more closely the natural world and to use their imagination to explain its unusual features. In this sense, the stories can be viewed as stimulating the development of scientific imagination.

The stories also encourage children to appreciate diverse cultural heritages from around the world. Indeed, we have designed the curriculum so that as children encounter a story from a particular region, they discover that it is present in other regions of the world. When children compare different versions of the same story, they come to appreciate not only diversity in human cultures but also a unity that holds them together at a deeper level. As Rugambwa-Otim has pointed out in Chapter 14, children need to become aware that they are citizens of the world as well as of their own country; stories of this kind are well designed to help them do so.

Stories from oral culture can also play an important role in second language learning. Indeed, they have a particular property that makes them uniquely suitable for this task. These stories are typically built around formulaic material that plays a crucial role in both plot and character development. As key formulas are repeated over and over, they function as a mnemonic device for both story tellers and listeners. Their role in nourishing memory was crucial in oral culture since no literate resources were available to keep the stories alive—either the teller and listener remembered the story or it disappeared.

The repetition of formulaic material can play a similarly crucial role for second language learners: they, too, must repeat material or it will vanish from their minds. Mere repetition of language is not, however, sufficient, as evidenced by the disappointing results of the audiolingual method that required learners to repeat structural patterns of language with virtually no attention to meaning. The value of repeating a formula within a story lies in the fact that it is intimately linked to meaning.

Let us now examine how the repetition of formulaic material works within a traditional story. The following story is adapted from Hottentot oral culture in South Africa (the repeated formula is italicised).

> The moon wanted to send humans a message and called the spider to be the messenger.
> *"Here is the message: 'As the moon dies and is reborn, so will humans die and be reborn.'"* The spider began its journey to bring the message to humans, but on its way it met a hare. The hare said: "Let me take the message. I am much faster than you."
> The spider agreed and said: *"Here is the moon's message: 'As the moon dies and is reborn, so will humans die and be reborn.'"*

The hare ran and ran with the message and finally reached the humans. The hare then said: *"Here is the moon's message: 'As the moon dies and is gone forever, so will humans die and be gone forever.'"*
The hare went back to the moon to tell her what it told the humans. The moon became angry and shouted: "How dare you tell humans a thing I have not said!" The moon grabbed a piece of wood and smashed the hare on the nose. This is why the hare's nose is slit.
Humans still believe the hare's message. That is why there is death in the world.

The formulaic material here consists of a message to be transmitted from the moon to humans. The message is passed on three times, from moon to spider, from spider to hare, and from hare to humans. In the final interaction, the hare, a creature whose speed is associated with carelessness, reverses the crucial elements in the message: the humans believe the distorted message, and so it becomes their fate. In the hare's reversal lies a peculiar irony, for just as the message from the moon to the humans depends upon exacting repetition of formulaic material, so the preservation of the story itself within oral culture depends upon comparably exacting repetition. In effect, not only humans but even stories die when formulaic material is not repeated with sufficient exactitude.

There is another feature that makes these stories valuable for teaching a second language: even though the language used is simple, the meaning is often complex. As the psycholinguist Pinker (1994) has pointed out, learners acquire language by a process known as "semantic bootstrapping": that is to say, as they work with accessible language, they are able to construct meaning that goes beyond what they ordinarily understand. Consider, for example, the Hottentot story. Apart from explaining why humans die (and, incidentally, why the hare has a slit nose), this story conveys a number of basic truths about communication such as

- a message tends to change as it is transmitted from one person to another;
- changes in a message often involve the reversal of lexical polarities (i.e. *reborn* becomes *gone forever*);
- a message is difficult to change once it has been imprinted.

This last truth is one that politicians and advertisers often exploit as they use the resources of mass communications. In effect, this apparently simple story opens up multiple worlds of meaning for a second language learner, whether child or adult, to explore.

In concluding this presentation, I would like to return to the title and the two epigraphs with which we began. As for the title, "To Read is To Write", we have seen how children create their own text as they read: as they integrate what they already know with what is on the page, they are, as it were, rewriting what is on the page. Such rewriting is fundamental to reading comprehension.

As for the epigraph from Lewis Carroll's *Alice's Adventures in Wonderland,* it conveys a basic point of this presentation—that text is enriched when it draws on oral resources. Alice is impatient with a book that lacks "pictures and conversation". Obviously she had graphic illustrations in mind when she said "pictures", but perhaps we can take the liberty of associating her use of this word with the images that story tellers create through words. If we do, we can then view her as having identified two basic resources of oral culture: at the heart of a story are images—the scenes in which the characters act and talk— and then there is, of course, the talk itself. Alice was right to want books that contain both image and talk.

The epigraph from Okot p'Bitek's *Song of Lawino* conveys another basic point that I would like to leave with you. If our teaching and testing suppresses creative reading, we end up deadening not only the texts that our students read but even the students themselves. Let us teach and test in such a way that our creative writers will no longer have to lament that reading kills those who attend our schools. Reading and writing creatively must be the theme not just of this conference but also of our classrooms.

References

Abadzi, H. (1994). *What we know about acquisition of adult literacy: Is there hope?* (World Bank Discussion Paper No. 245). Washington DC: The World Bank.

Alowo, J. (1997). *Our own English: Characteristics of Ugandan English. What do we want to teach our children?* Paper presented at the Ugandan German Cultural Society, Kampala, 30 January.

Bagunywa, A. (1980). *Critical issues in African education.*

Baker, J. N. (1993). The presence of the name: Reading scripture in an Indonesian village. In J. Boyarin (Ed.), *The ethnography of reading* (pp. 98-138). Berkeley: University of California Press.

Barton, D. (1994). *Literacy: An introduction to the ecology of written language.* Oxford: Blackwell.

Baynham, M. (1995). *Literacy practices: Investigating literacy in social contexts.* London: Longman.

Bloch, M. (1993). The uses of schooling and literacy in a Zafimanary village. In B. Street (Ed.), *Cross-cultural approaches to literacy* (pp. 87-109). Cambridge: Cambridge University Press.

Bright, J. A., & McGregor, G. P. (1970). *Teaching English as a second language.* London: Longman.

Carnegie, A. (1948). *Autobiography of Andrew Carnegie.* Boston: Northeastern University Press.

Carroll, L. (1962). *Alice's adventures in Wonderland.* London: Penguin. (Original work published 1865).

Carroll, L. (1962). *Through the looking glass.* London: Penguin. (Original work published 1872).

Chukovsky, K. (1963). *From two to five* (M. Morton, Trans.). Berkeley, CA: University of California Press.

Collins, J. (1986). Differential instruction in reading groups. In J. Cook-Gumperz (Ed.), *The social construction of literacy* (pp. 117-137). Cambridge: Cambridge University Press.

Cook, D. (1980). *African literature: A critical view.* London: Edward Arnold.

Cook, D. & Rubadiri, D. (Eds.) (1971). *Poems from East Africa.* London: Heinemann.

Cooper, R. (1989). *Language planning and social change.* London: Cambridge University Press.

Cox, C. A., & Dyson, E. A. (1982). *The practical criticism of poetry.* London: Edward Arnold.

Freire, P. (1972). *The pedagogy of the oppressed.* Harmsworth: Penguin.

Finnegan, R. (1976). *Oral literature in Africa.* Nairobi: Oxford University Press.

Galavaris, G. (1974). Teaching is giving yourself. In E. F. Sheffield (Ed.), *Teaching in the universities no one way* (pp. 1-8). Montreal and London: McGill-Queens University Press.

Gibson, D. (1996). Literacy, knowledge, gender and power in the workplace on three farms in the Western Cape. In M. Prinsloo & M. Breier (Eds.), *The social uses of literacy: Theory and practice in contemporary South Africa* (pp. 49-64). Philadelphia: John Benjamins.

Goody, J. (Ed.) (1968). *Literacy in traditional societies.* Cambridge: Cambridge University Press.

Goody, J. (1986). *The logic of writing and the organization of society.* Cambridge: Cambridge University Press.

Hammarskjeld, D. (1964). *Markings.* (L. Sjoberg & W. H. Auden, Trans.) London: Faber.

Heath, S. B. (1983). *Ways with words: Language, life, and work in communities and classrooms.* Cambridge: Cambridge University Press.

Hill, C. (1991). Recherches interlinguistiques en orientation spatiale. *Communications, 53,* 171–207.

Hill, C. (1992). *Testing and assessment: An ecological approach.* Inaugural lecture for the Arthur I. Gates Chair in Language and Education, New York: Teachers College, Columbia University.

Hill, C. (1995). Testing and assessment: An applied linguistics perspective. *Educational Assessment, 2,* 179-212.

Hill, C. & Langer de Ramirez, L. (1999). Why-stories from around the world. Unpublished manuscript.

Hill, C., & Larsen, E. (1999). *Children and reading tests.* Stamford, CT: Ablex Press.

Hill, C., & Parry, K. (1988). *Reading assessment: Autonomous and pragmatic models of literacy* (LC Report 88-2). New York: Teachers College, Columbia University, Literacy Center.

Hill, C., & Parry, K. (1989). Autonomous and pragmatic models of literacy: Reading assessment in adult education. *Linguistics and Education,* 1, 233-83.

Hill, C., & Parry, K. (1992). The test at the gate: Models of literacy in reading assessment. *TESOL Quarterly,* 26, 433-461.

Hill, C., & Parry, K. (Eds.) (1994). *From testing to assessment: English as an international language.* Harlow, UK: Longman.

The integrated syllabus and teacher's guide. (1983). Kampala: National Curriculum Development Centre.

Kagwa, A. (1912). *Ekitabo kya bika bya Buganda.* (The book of the clans of Buganda). Mengo: Kagwa's Hand-Press.

Kagwa, A. (1952). *Ekitabo kye mpisa za Buganda.* (The book of the traditions and customs of the Baganda). London: Macmillan.

Kagwa, A. (1953). *Basekabaka be Buganda.* (The Kings of Buganda). London: Macmillan.

Kajubi, W. S. (1989). *Education for national integration and development:* Report of Education Policy Review Commission. Kampala: Ministry of Education.

Kasozi, A. B. K. (1994). *The Social Origins of Violence in Uganda 1964-1985.* Montreal and Kingston: McGill-Queen's University Press.

Keshubi, H. (1997). *Going solo.* Kampala: Fountain Publishers.

Kiguli, S. (1998). *The African saga.* Kampala: Femrite.

Kyomuhendo, G. (1996). *The first daughter.* Kampala: Fountain Publishers.

Ladefoged, P., Glick, R., & Criper, C.. (Eds.). (1971). *Language in Uganda.* Nairobi: Oxford University Press.

Le Page, R. B. (1964). *The national language question: Linguistic problems of newly independent states.* London: Oxford University Press/ Institute of Race Relations.

MacGinitie, W. H. (1978). *Gates-MacGinitie Reading Tests* (2nd ed.). Boston: Houghton Mifflin.

Maddox, H. E. (1902). *An elementary Runyoro grammar.* London: Society for Promoting Christian Knowledge.

Mazrui, A. (1972). *Cultural engineering and nation-building in East Africa.* Evanston, IL: Northwestern University Press.

McArthur, T. (1998). *The English languages.* Cambridge: Cambridge University Press.

Michaels, S. (1986). Narrative presentations: an oral preparation for literacy with first graders. In J. Cook-Gumperz (Ed.), *The social construction of literacy* (pp. 94-116). Cambridge: Cambridge University Press.

Moody, H. L. B. (1987). *Literary appreciation. A practical guide.* London: Longman.

Mother tongue syllabus for primary schools. (1998). Kampala: National Curriculum Development Centre.

Mukama, R. (1989). The linguistic dimension of ethnic conflict. In K. Rupesinghe (Ed.) *Conflict resolution in Uganda.* London: James Currey.

Mukama, R. (1990). Language: A blue print for the integration of Uganda. *Makerere Papers in Languages and Linguistics,* 1 (1), 125-157.

Mukama, R. (1991). Recent developments in the language situation and prospects for the future. In H. B. Hansen & M. Twaddle (Eds.), *Changing Uganda: The dilemma of structural adjustment and revolutionary change* (pp. 334-50). London: James Curry.

Museveni, Y. K. (1997). *Sowing the mustard seed: The struggle for freedom and democracy in Uganda.* Basingstoke: Macmillan.

Nandwa, J. & Bukenya, A. (1983). *African oral literature for schools.* Nairobi: Longman Kenya.

Ndoleriire, O. (1990). Some aspects of the history of Runyoro-Rutooro. *Makerere Papers in Languages and Linguistics,* 1 (1), 19-47.

Ngologoza, P. (1967). *Kigezi n'abantu baamwo.* (Kigezi and its people). Nairobi: East African Literature Bureau.

Nsibambi, A. (1971). Language policy in Uganda: An investigation into costs and politics. *Journal of African Affairs,* 70, 62-71.

Nsibambi, A. (1991). *A report on the problems and prospects of national integration in Uganda, 1962-1991.*

Nsibambi, R. (1994). *Motivation of teachers of English: their conception of the problem.* Paper presented at the National English Conference, Makerere University, Kampala.

Ocwinyo, J. (1997). *Fate of the banished.* Kampala: Fountain Publishers.

O'Grady, B. (1974). Modest miracles do happen. In E. F. Sheffield (Ed.), *Teaching in the universities no one way* (pp. 18-29). Montreal and London: McGill-Queens University Press.

Okot p'Bitek. 1972. *Song of Lawino. Song of Ocol.* Nairobi: East African Publishing House.

Omoding-Okwalinga, J. (1985). *Literacy and the learning and practice of rural off-farm occupations.* Unpublished doctoral dissertation, University of Wisconsin, Madison.

Phillips, H. M. 1970. *Literacy and development.* Paris: UNESCO.

Pinker, S. (1994). *The language instinct.* Harmondsworth: Penguin.

Prinsloo, M., & Breier, M. (Eds.) (1996). *The social uses of literacy: Theory and practice in contemporary South Africa.* Philadelphia: John Benjamins.

Richards, J., Platt. J., and Weber, H. 1985. *Longman dictionary of applied linguistics.* Harlow: Longman.

Roberts, A. D. (1963). The sub-imperialism of the Baganda. *Journal of African History, 3* , 435-50.

Scribner, S., & Cole, M. (1981). *The psychology of literacy.* Cambridge, Mass: Harvard University Press.

Steinhart, E. I. (1999). *Conflict and collaboration: The kingdoms of Western Uganda 1890-1907.* Kampala: Fountain Publishers.

Street, B. V. (1984). *Literacy in theory and practice.* Cambridge: Cambridge University Press.

Street, B. V. (1995). *Social literacies: Critical approaches to literacy in development, ethnography, and education.* London: Longman.

Tiffen, B. (1969). *A language in common.* London: Longman.

Toolan, M. (1997). Recentering English: New English and Global English. *English Today,* 52, 3-9.

Tucker, A. R. (1970). *Eighteen years in Uganda and East Africa.* 2 volumes. Westport, CT: Negro University Press. (Original work published 1908)

Tucker, V. (1989). *Improve your memory, study and reading skills.* Bombay: Better Yourself Books.

Twaddle, M. (1974). Ganda receptivity to change. *Journal of African History,* 15, 303-15.

Twaddle, M. (1993). *Kakungulu and the creation of Uganda.* London: James Currey.

Uganda Government. (1992). *Government White Paper on implementation of the recommendation of the report of the Education Policy Review Commission.* Kampala: Author.

Uganda Government. (1993). *Constituent Assembly Statute.* Kampala: Author.

Uganda Government. (1995). *Constitution of the Republic of Uganda.* Kampala: Uganda Printing and Publishing Corporation.

UNESCO. (1996). *Learning: The treasure within.* Paris: UNESCO Publishing.

Wagner, D. A. (1993). *Literacy, culture, and development: Becoming literate in Morocco.* Cambridge: Cambridge University Press.

West, M. (1964). *A general service list of English words, with semantic frequencies and a supplementary word-list for the writing of popular science and technology.* London: Longman.

Whiteley, W. H. (1969). *Swahili: The rise of a national language.* London: Methuen.

Index

Achebe, Chinua 71, 90
Acholi 16, 44, 49, 98
Akaramojong 16, 48
Alowo, Jane 36, 63
Alur 16, 49
Amin, Idi 20, 26
Annual National Language and Literature
   Teaching Conference 1, 2
Arabic 30, 33, 63
Arabs 21, 30
area languages 41-43, 45, 48, 49, 53
assessment 82, 102, 105, 110, 111
Ateso 16, 25, 48, 49, 52

Bacon, Francis 9, 67
Bagunywa 46, 109
Bakahuuna, Elizabeth 58, 64, 71, 78, 79,
   92
Bakka, Peter 81, 83
Bantu languages 16, 20, 24-26, 3051, 52
Bitamazire, Ralph 95-96
Bornu 94
Bright 12, 67, 109
Britain 11, 18, 25
British Council 18
Bronte, Charlotte 71
Budo 6, 7, 9
Bukenya 93, 112
Bunyoro Kitara Development Foundation
   55
Byakutaga, Shirley 42, 45, 49, 51, 54, 63,
   65

Carnegie, Andrew 85, 109
Castle Report 53
CfBT 18
Chope 49
Columbia University 2, 105, 110

Congo 94
Constituent Assembly 2, 19, 26, 113
constitution of Uganda 1995 7, 19, 78
Cook, David 92-93, 96, 109
curriculum 2, 31, 47-49, 54, 58, 74,
   77-79, 80, 105, 106, 111, 112

Dhopadhola 16, 49
Dickens, Charles 12
District Language Boards 45

Education Commission 1987 See Kajubi
   Commission
Education Report 1948 52
English 1-4, 6, 7, 9-11, 12-13, 14, 15,
   17019, 21, 22, 24, 25, 26, 28-29, 34-
   40, 41, 42, 43-44, 45, 46, 54, 55, 58,
   59, 62-65, 67, 70, 72, 73, 74-76, 77-
   80, 82, 90, 91, 92, 96, 105, 109, 111,
   112, 113
English Literature 77
English literature 11, 73, 77

Finnegan 94, 110
Fisher, Pamela 15, 34
Fountain Publishers 111, 112, 113
Freire 64, 110
French 11, 30
functional illiteracy 83, 84
functional literacy 60, 83

General Service List of English Words 12,
   112
German 30, 33

Hausa 103
Hausaland 94

Hill, Clifford 2, 62, 64, 82, 96, 97, 98, 102, 103, 105, 110-111
Hottentot 106, 107
human rights 78, 79

illiteracy 58, 59, 60, 83, 84
in-Service education 34
In-Service Secondary Teacher Education Project (INSSTEP) 34
Integrated English 4
Integrated Syllabus the 37, 111
Islam 6, 26, 94
Institute of Teacher Education (ITEK) 31, 54-55
Izizinga, Rose 57-58, 65, 66

Jonam 49

Kafeero, Ibrahim 81-82, 92
Kagaba, Peter 9, 15, 30
Kagwa 65, 111
Kajubi Commission 1987 7, 10, 16, 17, 47, 66
Kakoba NTC 32, 62
Kampala district 44, 74
Kasozi, A.B.K. 8, 15, 17, 20, 23, 30, 42, 53, 64, 111
Kebu 49
Kenya 9, 24, 31-32, 63, 112
Kenyatta, Jomo 24
Keshubi, Hope 41, 43, 45, 46, 54, 64, 65, 80, 82
Kiguli 64, 74, 79, 80, 93, 111
Kinyara 43
Kiswahili 7, 9, 15, 17-18, 19-21, 22, 23-29, 30-33, 52, 53, 59, 61, 62, 63
Kiswahili Association of Uganda 32, 55
Kiwanuka, Basil 47
Kumam 16, 49

Kwikiriza, Loyce 73, 81-82, 88, 93, 96
Kyomuhendo, Goretti 111

Lango 16, 49
Language policy 16-22, 23-29
language policy 1, 7-9, 15, 16-22, 23-29, 41, 52, 112
Lendu 16, 49
Liberia 63
librarians 3, 4, 87
libraries 59, 61, 70, 81, 84-87, 105
literacy 1-4, 7, 16, 22, 24, 31, 44, 45, 52, 57-66, 69, 81-82, 83-87, 91, 96, 98, 109-113
literacy practices 57, 61, 63, 65, 81, 98, 109
literate culture 1, 97
literate skills 3-4, 47, 60, 65, 67, 83, 90, 91
literature 1-4, 6-7, 11, 24, 26, 28, 34, 44, 48, 50, 54-55, 57-58, 64, 67, 69, 71, 72, 73, 74, 75, 76, 77, 78, 79, 81, 82, 91, 92-93, 109, 110, 112
Literature in English 58, 74, 77-80, 82, 92
literature in English 4
local authorities 19
local councils 87
London School of Oriental and African Studies 77
Loro Teachers College 49
Lubwa p'Chong, Cliff 10
Luganda 15, 16, 20, 24, 25, 26, 28, 33, 43-45, 48, 49, 52, 55, 65, 93-95
Luganda Academy 55
Luganda Language Academy 28
Luganda Language Society 28
Lugbara 16, 25, 48, 52
Lunyoro 25, 52
Luo 16, 20, 25, 45, 48, 49, 71
Lusamya 43
Lusoga 16, 43
Luvuma 43

Madi 16, 48
Makerere University
  4, 6, 7, 8, 9, 10, 20, 32, 42,
  45, 47, 53, 54-56, 68,
  73, 84, 112
Makerere University School of Education
  6, 54
Makerere University Institute of Languages 4, 42
Mazrui, Ali 19, 20, 21, 22, 111
McGregor, Gordon 1, 6, 12, 17, 26,
  33, 67, 79, 109
medium of instruction 2, 3, 7, 17-18,
  23-28, 36, 43, 45, 46-47, 53
Ministry of Education and Sports
  2, 31, 47, 36, 54-55, 56, 66
missionaries 24-27, 52, 88, 94
Moody 92, 111
Morocco 63, 113
mother tongue 41-45, 46-50, 54, 56,
  62, 82, 92, 94, 95, 96
Mukama, Ruth 9, 10, 17, 20, 22, 28
multilingualism 15, 41, 44, 49, 82
Museveni, Yoweri 2, 9, 64
Musinguzi, Rwakisarale 42, 45, 49, 54, 63,
  65, 51

Nakaseke Teachers College 49
Nandwa, A 93, 112
National Curriculum Development Centre
  (NCDC) 31, 45, 54
national integration 2, 14, 16, 18-19, 22,
  29, 77, 78, 80, 111, 112
national language 1, 2, 8, 9, 14, 17-
  24, 26, 28, 46, 111, 113
National Resistance Movement (NRM)
  20, 23, 26, 27
National Teachers' Colleges 18, 31-32 35,
  47, 54
New York 2, 103, 110
New Zealand 6, 101
newspapers 15, 28, 37, 39, 55, 72, 83
Ngologoza 65, 112
Nilo-Hamitic languages 16
Nilotic languages 16
Ngugi wa Thi'ongo 71
Nsibambi, Apolo 1, 2, 17, 22, 112

Nsibambi, Rhoda 14, 16, 21, 26, 30, 42, 82
Nuffield Study Group, 1951-53 25
Nyerere, Julius 11

Obote, Milton 20
Ocwinyo, Julius 64, 112
ODA 18
official language 2, 10, 17, 18, 19,
  21, 36
Okot p'Bitek 71, 90, 95, 96, 97, 108, 112
Omoding-Okwalinga 60, 63, 112
oral culture 1, 58, 97, 98, 101, 103,
  105, 106, 107, 108
oral poetry 82
oral proficiency 3, 4
oral skills 4, 70, 91
oral traditions 4, 71, 88-91, 93-96
orality 4, 57, 81, 93, 96
orature 4, 72, 73, 81-82, 93-95
orthographies 4, 41, 44, 48, 52, 53
Oxford University Press 110, 111

Parry, Kate 57, 59, 66, 81, 98, 102,
  110-111
Pinker, Stephen 10, 107, 112

poetry 64, 82, 92-94, 96, 110
portfolios 105
Primary Education Reform 31, 41, 46
Primary Leaving Examination (PLE) 32
primary teacher education (PTE) 47
primary teachers colleges 31, 45, 46, 47-
  50
publishers 3, 4, 64, 84, 111-113

radio 28, 38, 50, 55, 57, 73
reading 1, 3, 4, 5, 11, 12, 37, 39,
  47, 57, 58, 60-71, 74, 75-76,
  79, 80-87, 89-91, 97-103, 105,
  108, 109, 110, 111, 113
reading culture 4, 69, 74, 81-82. 89
Roscoe, Reverend John 26
Rowlings, Reverend 26

Rugambwa-Otim 58, 64, 73, 77
Runyakitara 42, 45, 48-49, 51, 52-56
Runyankore-Rukiga 16, 51-55,65, 82,
    88-91
Runyoro 51-54, 111, 112
Runyoro-Rutooro 51, 53, 54, 112
Rutooro 51, 52, 53, 54, 96, 112
Rwabushaija, Milton 62
Sanyu, Florentina 41, 43, 48
Snoxall, R.A. 52, 53
Sotho 94
South Africa 63, 106, 110, 112
Ssemuju, Herman 84
Standard English 37, 39, 40
standard English 37, 38
Sudanic languages 16
Support for Uganda Primary Education
    Reform (SUPER) 31, 41, 48-40

Tanzania 9, 17, 19, 31, 32
Teacher Development and Management
    Systems (TDMS) 31, 48-49
teacher resource centres (TRCs) 34-35
television 28, 50, 55, 57
Tiffen, Brian 17
translation 54, 65, 95

Tucker, Bishop 26
Uganda Edvanced Certificate of Education
    32
Uganda Certificate of Education 32-33
Uganda Language Society 20
Uganda National Examinations Board
    (UNEB) 7, 32-33
Uganda People's Congress 20
Ugandan English 36-37, 109
UNESCO 60, 80, 112, 113
United States Information Agency 2, 18
United States Information Service 2
United States of America 18, 25, 84, 98
Universal Primary Education (UPE) 21
USAID 18, 48
Voice of Tooro 55

White Paper on education 7, 17-17, 23, 26-
    28, 31-32, 41, 42, 43-44, 47, 53,
    57, 59,61, 6264, 69, 78
World Bank 48, 109
World War 25

Zulu 94